D0338800

RIVER DAYS

AMERICAN ALPINE CLUB LIBRARY
710 10th ST., SUITE 15
GOLDEN, CO 80401
(303) 384-0112

RIVER DAYS

TRAVELS ON WESTERN RIVERS

A COLLECTION OF ESSAYS

Jeff Rennicke, Contributing Editor

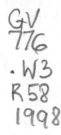
GV
776
.W3
R58
1998

Copyright © 1988
Jeff Rennicke

Book and Jacket Design
Richard Firmage

Cover Photograph
Tom Beck

All rights reserved.

"Colorado River: Grand Canyon," "Colorado River: Westwater Canyon," "Rio Chama," "Rogue River" and "Yampa River" originally appeared in slightly different form in *River Runner*.

"Colorado River: Horsethief Canyon," "Gunnison River Gorge," "Kobuk River" and "Tuolumne River" originally appeared in slightly different form in *Canoe*.

Library of Congress Cataloging-in-Publication Data

River days.

1. Boats and boating—West (U.S.)
2. Rivers—West (U.S.)—Recreational use.
I. Rennicke, Jeff.

GV776.W3R58   1988   797.1'0978   88-3821
           ISBN 1-55591-029-7

1 2 3 4 5 6 7 8 9 0

Fulcrum, Inc.
Golden, Colorado
1988

This book is dedicated to that anonymous paddler who first uttered the wise words, "Even a bad day on the river is better than a good day at work."

ACKNOWLEDGMENTS

For many years the art of writing about rivers, like the sport of running them, has been overlooked and neglected. It was, some editors and publishers thought, just the scratchings of a bunch of weather-beaten boatmen trying to fill in the time between trips and to raise a little beer money.

Today both river writing and river running are coming into the mainstream. For all the writers represented in this book I would like to thank Darby Junkin, Hunter Holloway, Robert Baron, Betsy Armstrong and all the people of Fulcrum for believing enough in river writing and the people who do it to put a book like this together.

Thanks to Jerry Mallett, Tom Beck and Jill Wolf-Rennicke who read parts of this manuscript, offered suggestions and shared so many of the river trips in the book.

Finally, I would like to thank the people at *Canoe* and *River Runner* magazines. Many of the chapters of this book appeared in slightly different form in the pages of these two magazines. For many years these publications have been the only outlet for river writers, giving us a place to publish, a place to practice our craft and sometimes even helping us to raise a little beer money along the way.

J.R.

PREFACE
A WORLD OF RIVER STORIES
Jerry Mallett
Executive Director
Western River Guides Association

River running has become a mainstream recreational event. Once a challenge for only a few world explorers, today individuals of all ages, walks of life and physical skills enjoy river trips throughout the United States and the world. While trips vary from a half-day to three weeks or longer, the reasons people come to the river are even more diverse: wildlife photography, big water adventure, relaxing floats beneath a blue sky, personal challenge alone on a river in a kayak.

Whatever it is that brings people to the water, river running opportunities have grown dramatically over the last decade. New advances in outdoor clothing, safety equipment, boating gear and the growing skills of paddlers have all opened up new and wild horizons everyone can now share.

This is a book about those horizons. River tales, whether told around a campfire or in the pages of magazines and books, have played a large part in the growing interest in river running. Finally, here is a collection of these tales. Everyone, whether looking for a first river trip or a new adventure, will find a river to dream about within these pages. It is just around the bend.

TABLE OF CONTENTS

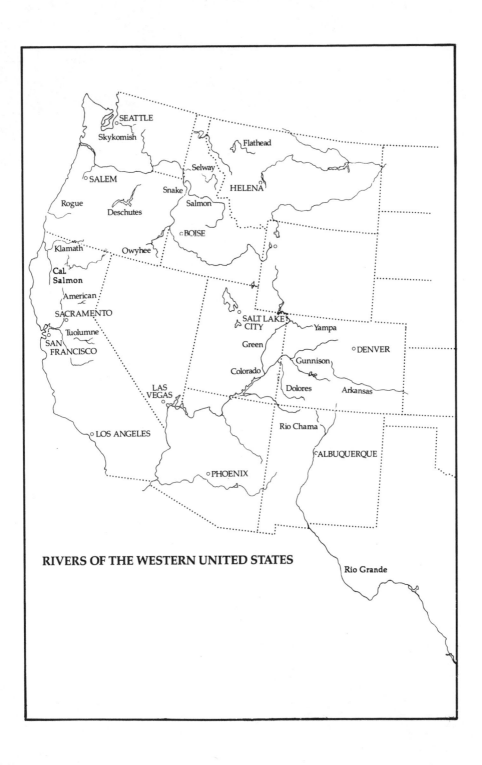

SEATTLE
Skykomish
Flathead
Selway
SALEM
HELENA
Snake
Rogue
Salmon
Deschutes
BOISE
Klamath
Owyhee
Cal.
Salmon
American
SACRAMENTO
SALT LAKE
CITY
Yampa
Tuolumne
Green
DENVER
SAN
FRANCISCO
Colorado
Gunnison
LAS
VEGAS
Dolores
Arkansas
LOS ANGELES
Rio Chama
ALBUQUERQUE
PHOENIX

RIVERS OF THE WESTERN UNITED STATES

Rio Grande

INTRODUCTION
THE SEARCH FOR
THE PERFECT RIVER

Night. The campfire has burned low, just a string of pale, gray smoke braiding as it rises. The stars, like sparks, have risen over the canyon walls. The moon is still a long way off. Down at the river, one of the boatmen is securing the rafts for the night and snaps the lid on a riverbox. The echo cracks against the canyon walls, then again more distant, once more and is gone.

The conversation around the campfire is quiet but serious, laced with words like *endo*, *brace* and *highside* and sprinkled with terms like *upstream ferry angle* and *catching an eddy*. There are stories of places with strange names like Black Rocks, the Gates of Lodore, Elves Chasm, Jackass Flat, Tiger Wall and Chili Bar. There are tales of tall spires of rock called hoodoos, of hot springs where the steam rises like spirits over the blue-green water and of thousand-year-old petroglyphs carved into canyon walls where the silence is older than the rock.

And there is the whitewater, always the whitewater. Warm Springs, Zoom Flume, Snaggletooth, Skull, Redside, Hells-Half-Mile, The Vortex, Clavey Falls, Big Drop, Crystal and Lava Falls. When the voices trail off, even for just a moment, from beyond the circle of light there come the faint sounds of a river flowing.

The camp is on a river—the Dolores, the Rogue, the Colorado, the Salmon, it makes little difference—and the talk is of rivers, but not just any river. It is of the *perfect* river. It happens every time, usually late in the trip or at the last camp. As surely as water flows downhill, put two or more river runners around a campfire and the talk will turn to the perfect river. Every paddler is searching for it.

1

Like the surfer's perfect wave, you can see it in their eyes by the light of the fire or at the sight of moving water.

The standards are tough—wilderness, scenery, access, whitewater, history, challenge, wildlife, solitude, good camps, archaeology, gradient, water quality, fishing. The good boatmen carry a checklist in their heads the way baseball fans memorize the National League batting averages. For some, it becomes an obsession, like the Holy Grail or the Northwest Passage. For some, it is a cause worth defending around a lifetime of campfires, or a reason to dream and wait it out through another long winter. For others it is an excuse to pump up the boat, patch the kayak and spend long nights tracing with their fingers the thin blue lines of rivers on the topographic maps.

The maps are a good place to start. A quick glance at a map of the western United States gives the impression that this is hardly the place to start looking for a river, any river, let alone the *perfect* river. Beyond the fabled "dry line" of the 100th meridian, precipitation levels trail off like an echo in a box canyon. With little water from the skies, there are few rivers for the land. The map of the West is not tangled with blue lines like other places where the time between rainstorms is measured in days, not months.

But the dots on the maps, the cities, are also few and far between, so what rivers there are carry wide horizons on their banks and stretch out like snakes in the morning sun. It is pure space where the horizons shimmer with the slow ache of distance. The drainages of some western rivers could encircle entire states in the East. They are solitary, untamed, wild.

Here are the epic journeys, the long runs like the three-week Grand Canyon trips, the week-long Yampa trips, the endless days of floating through Stillwater and Labyrinth canyons on the lower Green, the hundred miles of the Klamath. It is here in the West where you can come to know whole rivers, not just chopped-up sections, and float a river like Idaho's Middle Fork of the Salmon from its headwaters to its mouth. There is a completeness in running a whole river, start to finish, like hearing a whole song instead of just a few short notes.

Here too are the wild rivers. Shooting off the Rockies or out of the Sierras like short fuses come rivers that are as hard to tame as the land they flow through. This wildness has not gone unrecognized. To date, 75 percent of the rivers designated in the National Wild and Scenic Rivers System can be found in Alaska, Idaho and California.

California has the most designated rivers outside of Alaska; Colorado has the most miles studied, recommended and awaiting designation.

The roll call is the stuff of legend—the Cache la Poudre, the Rogue, the Middle Fork of the Feather, the Middle Fork of the Salmon, the Tuolumne, the Rio Grande, the Skagit, the Flathead, the Trinity, the Clearwater and on and on, names that flow off the tongue like water slipping over rocks. And the names of those that should be in the National Wild and Scenic Rivers System but, as yet, are not: the Dolores, the Yampa, the Gunnison, the Priest and the Bruneau. Lay a compass on any piece of slickrock in the West and chances are that every last heading will point to a wild river.

Yet, the western rivers have not escaped the onslaught of water projects and problems. In a land where rain is more precious than gold, rivers are the only game in town for the thirsty cities, the dusty rows of irrigation ditches, the lawn sprinklers that chatter in the cities. A toll has been taken.

No river so reflects this toll as clearly as the blood vein of the West, the Colorado River. It is being sucked dry. The Bureau of Reclamation alone boasts 333 reservoirs, 990 miles of pipeline, 345 diversion dams, 14,590 miles of canals and 230 miles of tunnel that pull, push, suck, draw and divert the water of the Colorado River and its tributaries out of the river and into the garden hoses and hot tubs of places like Los Angeles, Denver, Phoenix, Las Vegas. This perpetual drain continues unclogged until the Colorado River itself, taxed beyond its measure, flows off into the ground as thick as spit 20 miles short of its mouth at the Gulf of California.

The Colorado is only a single chapter in what has been a long legacy of abuse. Part of the Upper Dolores River was stilled in 1983 when the Bureau of Reclamation closed the gates on the McPhee Dam, one of the newest of its arsenal. Others, like San Francisco's 1923 O'Shaughnessy Dam on the Tuolumne, the only major dam within the boundaries of a national park, and the Hoover Dam completed in 1936, are shadows of a different era and a different way of looking at the landscape. They are remnants of a time when it was believed that rain would follow the plow and, even if not, the rivers could make the western deserts bloom.

But we are coming to an end of that era, of that way of looking at the landscape. Our rivers are stretched thin and what remains has sparked an understanding in us—that perhaps our wild rivers are a valuable natural resource when left to flow free. Rivers are ribbons that tie us to the spirit of the land. Some of those ribbons must be left uncut; the long legacy of abuse must end.

On those wild rivers that do remain, river runners can discover that even for all the long years of abuse the beauty of rivers is an even longer legacy. Between the dams, the western rivers have held on to their beauty. The Gunnison River, below the triple choke-hold of the Curecanti Project, is still one of the most beautiful expressions of flowing water in the West. Powell and his men would still feel the twang in their guts as they approached the rapid they named Hells-Half-Mile on the Green despite Flaming Gorge Dam upstream. The last unthrottled stretch of the Tuolumne was finally protected by the National Wild and Scenic Rivers System in 1984. And some rivers remain that have never known diversions—the Middle Fork of the Salmon in Idaho, the Yampa in Colorado and others. They still flow free.

Despite our worst efforts—salinization, toxic chemical spills, diversions, pipelines, tunnels—mankind has not yet succeeded in wringing all the magic and beauty from the rivers of the West. Dams don't last forever. The rivers, they are patient.

Attracted to the beauty and wildness that remain on western rivers, the paddlers come to the riverbanks in greater numbers each year, making river running one of the fastest-growing outdoor sports in the West. Sometimes the numbers are staggering.

In 1965, only 547 people rafted the Colorado River through the Grand Canyon. Just seven years later, the river was floated by 16,432 people and only the institution that year of a permit system kept the numbers from climbing higher. It is estimated that more than 120,000 people paddled Colorado's Arkansas River in 1987. Another 100,000 ran the South Fork of the American in California. Strict permit systems similar to the one used in the Grand Canyon are the only things keeping similar numbers away from rivers like the Middle Fork of the Salmon, the Yampa and the Tuolumne.

Anyone can run a river and there are rivers for all types of paddlers. Trips range from mild quietwater to wild whitewater, from just a few hours on the water, to a few days, to several weeks. There are trips for the elderly, kids, and for special populations of the handicapped, for groups of all women or all men, for singles and for families, and for groups of fishermen. There are places to go solo and there are even the now-famous "float and bloat" trips that offer gourmet cuisine for the more sophisticated palates among us. The river plays no favorites. With the advent of safe rafts that can carry coolers full of fresh food and camping equipment, rivers have become the pathway to the wilderness for everyone. Yet, there are still rivers where a lone kayaker can slip into the current at dawn and float downstream solo, drifting as quietly as a raven feather.

People come for the sunshine. They come for the wilderness. They come for the fishing. But mostly, they come for the whitewater. The International Whitewater Rating System classifies rapids on a scale of I to VI. A Class I rapid is just moving water; Class II entails waves up to 3 feet with a clear channel; Class III is the beginning of the roar, 5-foot waves with boulders and obstacles to wind around; Class IV is considered heavy water, many obstacles, big waves and the start of butterflies for most western boatmen; Class V is on the edge, requiring extreme moves and precise boat-handling; it is the realm of only the most skilled; Class VI is the end of the line, unrunnable, portage time.

Some boaters look to a river's gradient for a clue to its whitewater, but the gradient, which is a measure of how many feet per mile a river drops, is only an average over the entire length of the run. Even a more specific gradient for a specific rapid is only part of the story because it leaves out things like boulders in mid-stream. Still, it is a number, something to start with.

Because the numbers are only a guide, it is always best to stay within your own limits and within your own judgment regardless of what the numbers tell you. All the numbers go out the window when you step to the edge of a major rapid for the first time.

Whitewater is the summit—the peak—of river running and it is unlike anything else in the world of sports. Shooting rapids is a one-shot deal, the muzzleloader of water sports. Unlike fishing, where you can reel in and try another cast, or rock climbing, where you can rappel down and try another route, whitewater requires that you get it right the first time. There is no reeling back a kayak, no reloading. You scout, plan, plan again and go.

First comes the roar of the water in the tight canyon, a sound like distant thunder, followed by the straining of the boatmen to see over the drop. The boat then seems to float out onto the tongue, a strangely quiet, slick spot where things go calm and smooth at the head of every rapid, like a lull before the storm—that first wave. Your heart pounds, your fists clench and you are in it: whitewater.

Just as suddenly you are out, floating gently in the tailwaves below, where the waves settle like a song fading to silence. You look back over your shoulder as the boat drifts around the bend. And you think back, reliving every wave, every moment, for the first of what will be thousands of times. Somewhere far downstream, you notice your heart is still racing and your fists are still clenched.

But a river is more than whitewater and there are other things to experience—deer feeding quietly in the shadows along the shore, old cabins where the wind whistles through the broken slits like the voices of old miners, a natural hot springs on the Middle Fork of the Salmon. All things to add to the checklist for the perfect river.

The talk around the campfire ebbs for a moment. On the wind there comes the sound of the river. The moon has risen. Someone stokes the fire, stirring the coals to life, and, as the flames rise, another river story begins. As long as there are wild rivers and people who paddle them, there will be stories.

This is a book of those stories, told by the paddlers who know them best, who know the rivers and have been there in the rapids and on the quietwater. These are the stories that keep us coming back to the water's edge and keep us huddling around the campfire late at night. One more story to tell before the campfire burns low, one more bend in the river to paddle before the sun sets. It is all a part of that endless pursuit, the search for the perfect river.

Jeff Rennicke
Boulder, Colorado

THE AMERICAN RIVER

SOUTH FORK

David Bolling

Location: Northern California
Whitewater: Class II-III
River Miles: 19
Gradient: 25 feet per mile
Trip Length: 1 to 2 days
Permit Required: Yes
Contact: Bureau of Land Management
63 Natoma Street, Fullerton, CA 95630
(916) 925-4434

Put-In Point: Chili Bar
Take-Out Point:
Salmon Falls Bridge
Access: San Francisco, CA
Sacramento, CA
Land Status: BLM, private

It is the K-Mart of California rivers: 19 miles of low-budget whitewater with easy accessibility, plenty of parking and hordes of consumers shopping for cheap thrills. There are no blue-light specials here, but when the dam at Chili Bar releases extra water there's a stampede to the put-in that rivals a checkout line the day before Christmas.

It's a fairly easy, often crowded river, and experienced boaters with Class V credentials sometimes describe it with overtones of bored disdain, like Macy's regulars talking down the virtues of K-Mart. But even the hotdogs keep coming back. If you press them for reasons, you discover that they really need this place, that California's best boaters probably spend more time on the water here than anywhere else.

Maybe that's because this is a river with a little something for almost everyone: rapids you can drive to and play in all day,

7

stretches of almost-wilderness where golden eagles still soar, long
tranquil pools where kids can pan for gold, a deep granite gorge and
one dramatic S-shaped drop surrounded by bedrock bleacher seats
where spectators congregate like fans at a football game to cheer (or
jeer) each boat through.

There are campgrounds and riverside parks positioned at stra-
tegic points and a very special vein of history that runs deep along
each bank. It's the original river of gold, El Dorado, the place the gold
rush began, the South Fork of the American.

In Northern California the South Fork is a whitewater mecca. It
is a place where neophytes come to worship at the altar of Odin, a
place where hundreds of thousands of commercial river passengers
have experienced their first whitewater. But still it is a place where
experts congregate to refine their skills.

Like K-Mart, the South Fork is accessible, popular and cheap.
One hour from Sacramento, three hours from San Francisco, the
river flows out of the foothills of the Mother Lode to within easy
reach of more than five million people. It abounds with commercial
companies and competition keeps the price of one- and two-day
trips reasonable.

Competition also drives outfitters to offer extra-cost options like
gourmet meals and stopovers in historic gold rush hotels. And
because its rapids are relatively kind, beginning boaters can safely
survive without investing the mortgage money in expensive equipment. All manner of rafts are in evidence here, from the latest self-
bailing SuperTech to your basic K-Mart rubber ducky.

The price of so much popularity, of course, is congestion, and on
some summer weekends it might almost be easier to walk the
American—on an inflated highway of Hypalon—than to boat it. At
some popular rapids, traffic management has become a necessity
and it is not uncommon, on a Saturday afternoon in July, to find a
whistle-blowing boater playing traffic cop at the big hole in First
Threat, where hotdoggers sometimes park their kayaks for extended
periods of play. River-use studies indicate more than 100,000 people
float the South Fork each year, making it one of the two or three most
traveled whitewater rivers in the nation. And while veteran kayakers who have graduated upward to the Tuolumne, the Merced or the
Kern may not consider the South Fork a challenge, drop by Chili Bar
hole any weekend and you'll find even the best of them waiting in
line to practice 360s, pop-ups and hand rolls.

Chili Bar, a misspelled reference to Chilean miners who worked the South Fork's gravel for gold, is the top of the run. Half a mile downstream the American leaves civilization behind as it enters a steep-walled canyon and careens through a quarter-mile rock garden named Meatgrinder. At low water Meatgrinder is a lengthy slalom course, at high water a thundering procession of deep holes and standing waves. Novice kayakers bomb straight downsteam, flailing paddles as fast as they can, while experienced boaters carve the rapid into dozens of ferries and eddy turns. Rafters row furiously left or right to avoid the infamous can opener rock at the bottom.

, For five miles the South Fork follows a winding, westerly course, alternating between a succession of short drops, several long rocky rapids and peaceful stretches of flatwater where modern day miners suck gravel and gold off the riverbed with small floating dredges. Then the river plunges over a granite ledge at Troublemaker, maybe the single most popular rapid in America. If you're part of a first-time paddle crew, primed with anxiety for the South Fork's worst drop, worried about flipping in the big hole or wrapping on the current-splitting rock below it, you may be startled to find a gallery of viewers waiting to witness your every move. Now is not a time to clutch. But if you do, at least three professional photographers, shooting both still and video cameras, are positioned on the adjoining rocks with signboards announcing the number of your run so that you can later buy a graphic record of your achievement. You can not run Troublemaker on the sly except in mid-week, late in the day.

Beyond Troublemaker, the river relaxes for a while and pools up beside one of the more significant sites in American history. On the left bank a stone monument marks the original position of Sutter's Mill where, on January 24, 1848, James Marshall found gold nuggets in the tailrace of a sawmill, sparking the great gold rush and the subsequent Americanization of California. A rebuilt mill occupies higher ground in a state park alongside the river and relics of the gold era are scattered within easy walking distance around the mill.

The gold rush rearranged the American River almost as much as it rearranged California. Within the year after Marshall found those fateful nuggets, a riverside community named Coloma had exploded into life with 13 hotels, two breweries and a proportional number of saloons, gambling halls and brothels. At its height the town had 10,000 residents, all drawn directly or indirectly by the mesmerizing allure of gold. Coloma is now a sleepy—if tourist-trod—village, but the American River carries permanent scars from the impact of all those people. At Coloma the river is a lake, its bed gouged into a giant pool by dredges. Elsewhere the channel has been straightened or bent, water forced one way or another to expose the gravels that fed the endless appetite for gold. Below Coloma there is a gentle rapid named Old Scary which didn't exist before the gold rush and almost doesn't exist now. It took shape when miners forced the river to the right over a rock ledge. The result was a seething hole that surprised and excited boaters for years until a recent flood shifted it again, stranding the ledge high and dry and reducing the rapid once more to a few mild waves.

Between Coloma and Lotus (another gold rush mining town) the American offers four miles of Class II river that have become an obligatory training run for beginning boaters. Mild rapids and a few good surging waves carry paddlers past more gold rush relics and an increasing number of private homes. Here the American is almost an urban river, threading a fine line between public and private rights. Over the years, the screams and whoops from exuberant rafters, filling the space between rapids with bail-bucket fights, have conflicted with the riverside peace and quiet sought by riparian land owners. To maintain harmony, a management plan was adopted which imposes a quiet zone along the most heavily populated part of the river and attempts to limit each boating group to a manageable size. Below Lotus, long stretches of public land restore the sense of wilderness and allow access to the shore for overnight camping.

The river remains calm for several miles, winding lazily through the foothills with a little Class II action as it builds for the grand finale. Then, with only three miles left before the still waters of Folsom Reservoir swallow it, the South Fork drops into the American River Gorge, a deep bedrock defile carved into a succession of lively Class III rapids. Knowledgeable river runners know the gorge is near when they spot the Lolly-pop tree, a lone pine crowning the top of a bald hill. The Lolly-pop disappears twice as the river meanders. The third time you see it, the gorge gathers up its granite flanks and invites you into a chasm of pulsing whitewater and sculpted rock. The rapids are sprinkled with names that heighten the drama for first-time visitors—Satan's Cesspool, Dead Man's Drop, Haystack Canyon, Bouncing Rock and Hospital Bar. But even here, in what now feels like the hard, raw face of nature, man has been mucking about. The gorge was once much rockier, perhaps impassible for rafts at today's low summer flows. But determined entre-preneurs sought to make a giant flume out of the South Fork to trans-port lumber from the Georgetown Divide downriver to Sacramento. To do that, they dumped tons of black powder into the river, trying to blow it clear of obstructions. They never succeeded in making the American a successful waterway for loggers, but they certainly cleared the way for whitewater boaters, most of whom are blissfully unaware that the narrow walls of the gorge once shook with mighty explosions. It's graphic evidence that the power and resilience of the river makes the scars from the blasting all but invisible now.

There are many faces to the South Fork, from raucous whitewa-ter freeway to wilderness refuge. But if you want to experience it at its most sublime, you have to visit it at night, under a full moon, when the deer come down out of the hills to sip delicately from its banks and beaver cruise through quiet eddies, carving V-waves in the still water. In the spring, when snowmelt keeps the river high enough to cover the more innocuous rocks, a night-time trip through the gorge is magic. Moonlight provides definition to the river's flow and the silence that descends in the dark will highlight sounds you never hear during the day. The rapids seem somehow softer at night, almost caressing as you slide a kayak through moonlit foam.

But even the daytime crush of boaters serves the South Fork well. Their numbers have given the river a powerful constituency which has thus far managed to preserve it from the endless schemes of dam builders and hydro-power mongers. State legislation offers the South Fork temporary protection from on-stream dam develop-ment, and an ambitious water diversion project has been killed that would have de-watered much of the river. To those who worry that a river can be overused and loved to death, the South Fork of the American is enduring evidence that, with proper management and a lot of public support, even one of the most popular whitewater rivers in America can retain its integrity and remain a living treasure.

2

THE ARKANSAS RIVER

BROWNS CANYON

Jeff Rennicke

Location: Southeastern Colorado
Whitewater: Class II-III
River Miles: 11
Gradient: 30 feet per mile
Trip Length: 1 day
Permit Required: No

Put-In: Fisherman's Bridge
Take-Out: Hecla Junction
Access: Buena Vista, CO
         Salida, CO
Land Status: Private,
         Bureau of Land Management

Contact: Bureau of Land Management
         Royal Gorge Resource Area, P.O. Box 1470
         Canon City, CO 81212
         (303) 275-7578

Dawn. The valley is still. The only movement is the mist drifting slowly like the dust of far-off riders coming nearer. The first light of day is the color of new ice and seems so beautiful and fragile that it would shatter at the first snap of an ammo can lid or the whine of an electric air pump. There is snow on the peaks, new snow, so brilliantly white against the first rays of the sun that it stings my eyes to stare too long at the summits. From just below and out of sight, there come the soft sounds of a river moving.

At times like these, mornings in early June, this place seems brand new, right out of the package. At 5 o'clock in the morning it is hard to believe that the Arkansas River is one of the busiest whitewater rivers in the West with more than 120,000 paddlers a year. By mid-morning the parking lot at Fisherman's Bridge will be buzzing with the music of air pumps and ammo cans, and the ground will look as if a rainbow has fallen from the sky and shattered into a hundred pieces—red Achilles, orange Rogue Rivers, gray Avons, sky-blue Argonauts, yellow Maravias, even a few old black Udiscos.

The names on the sides of the rafts and kayaks will look like a character list from a new *Star Wars* movie—Willowa, Spirit, Santanna, Sotar, Riken, Havasu, Dancer, Mustang, Mirage. But it is not an invasion, just a typical day on one of the premier whitewater rivers in these parts—the Arkansas River.

But all of that is still a few hours off. For now, there is only the river flowing cold and blue, the color of the sky over the peaks. I shiver once to shake off the cold and walk to the water. It seems the perfect place for a river, nestled in the long, wide arms of the Arkansas Valley of Colorado and guarded by the high summits of the 14,000-foot Collegiate Peaks to the west, the rolling hills of the Mosquito Range to the east and the first of the Sangre de Cristo Mountains which billow like storm clouds over the horizon to the south.

The Arkansas is a mountain river whose source is in the sky. The first trickle of what will become the Arkansas is born in the snowmelt on Mount Elbert which, at 14,433 feet, is the highest point in Colorado and the second-highest in the contiguous 48 states.

The Arkansas is a canyon river. In its first 125 miles, the river tumbles more than 5,000 feet. The power in that falling water has cut a series of deep canyons. Some are famous among the motorhome and postcard crowd like the narrow slot of Royal Gorge with its suspension bridge strung across it like a hair dangling 1,053 feet above the river, making it the world's highest. Recently people have begun paddling the Royal Gorge, a place of dark shadows, steep walls and Class IV rapids stacked end to end like the boxcars of a runaway train. Other rapids, like the Numbers, are best known to kayakers who call the six-mile run upstream of the town of Buena Vista "the very definition of Class IV."

The Arkansas is a plains river winding out onto the flats at the mouth of its last canyon more than a mile lower than its headwaters. At the town of Holly it leaves Colorado and begins a long, slow meander through wheat fields and prairie towns to the Mississippi River and the sea.

The Arkansas is a river of many faces—the Numbers the gorge; the Parkdale Run; the Cotopaxi Run, which is the course for the oldest whitewater kayak race on the continent; Pine Creek, which hides in its heart one of the most furious Class V rapids in the West.

From flatwater to extreme whitewater, the Arkansas is a collection of runs that could keep a paddler busy and challenged for years and which has earned the town of Buena Vista, the self-proclaimed title of "Whitewater Capital of Colorado." For most, however, the name *Arkansas River* means one thing—Browns Canyon.

The hoard has arrived. At 10 o'clock in the morning the sun is blasting the valley floor. The heat is up. The mountains seem to have pulled back and the day has broken. Fisherman's Bridge looks like the arrival of the Barnum and Bailey Big Top—buses, tents, mountains of rubber being inflated like elephants rising on command. It's show time.

We push off just ahead of a group of 30 Texans carrying their flotilla of rafts to the water on their shoulders. With all of them dressed in the same blue raingear and wearing the same orange life jackets, they look like the larvae of some strange insect making for the water.

The river gives us little time to gawk. From the start, the Arkansas is a busy river. It is early in the year and the river is running at medium levels, about 2,000 cubic feet per second. Still, the channel is toothed with rocks, play spots for the kayakers, early practice for the paddleboaters. Since it is a busy run with good current the whole way through, Browns Canyon is well-suited for paddleboats and kayaks. Oarboats, on this part of the river, are few and far between.

We have five boats on this trip—four paddleboats and an oarboat. Bill Dvorak, Reed Dils and Rick Medrick captain three of the paddleboats. Jerry Mallett, executive director of the Western River Guides Association, is at the oars. All of them know the river. The other paddleboat, which I captain on just my third Arkansas trip, has done the least number of trips here and does most of the rockin' and rollin' on this one.

Things slip by quickly—Oracle Bar, Ruby Mountain Riffle, Dead Tree Riffle, the fish hatchery. Running the Arkansas for the first time is like watching a movie in fast-forward or listening to the Beatles' *White Album* backwards. Very little makes sense. There are so many moves, so many rocks. That is part of the excitement. Once you are in, you're in. It is not until four miles downstream that we can finally pull over and top-off the rafts which have gone soft splashing in the cold water. Even though the air is hot, the water is as cold as ice.

A hard boat bounces better and that can be important because just downstream lies the first major rapid, appropriately named

Pinball. It is a right bend in the river strewn with rocks, a highly technical run where first bounces count. Pinball has been the site of some of the most creative lines on the river with boats careening off rocks and spinning like, well, pinballs. At low water it is a bit like paddling through a talus slope. At medium water, like today, there are just enough slots to make me think we might get through cleanly. Then, with just a few moves left, we hit hard on a rock. The force of the current swings us off and we backpaddle the rest of the way out to where the water settles.

It does not settle for long. On the Arkansas there are not many spaces between the songs of the rapids. Just over a half-mile downstream, around a blind corner, the river is squeezed and seems to drop off a cliff—Zoom Flume. This is the heart of the Browns Canyon run. This is the river's crescendo.

The boat drops in smoothly, aimed right on the V of the tongue of the smooth water before the first drop. On the other Arkansas trips I've taken, we've always stopped and done the long, hot walk down the railroad tracks on river left to scout Zoom Flume. But there is a controversy about what the railroad company sees as "trespass" on its right-of-way and so we don't scout this time. We just go.

It is all right with me. Scouting seems to interrupt the more natural flow than in just running a rapid. At different water levels Zoom Flume can change drastically, but on the medium water of early summer it is a right-hand run all the way.

The first wave is a reflection wave off the right wall that snaps the boat at a funny angle, but once we are up and over that and lined up straight, the river seems to do all the work. Deep in the troughs between waves, the light seems to filter through the water as it wouldthrough the prisms of a diamond. I think for just a second about the Apache Tears, the beautiful slivers of rock found scattered around Ruby Mountain upstream, until another rock, this time the Pyramid Rock that marks the end of Zoom Flume, comes into view. We are safely to the right of the Pyramid. The big waves are behind.

Since Browns Canyon is such a short run, we stop for a long lunch just downstream from Zoom Flume. It is our first chance to really look around. Browns Canyon has been called a "carnival run" and there is no doubt that most of the paddlers come to the river for the whitewater. But the canyon has its moments of scenery as well.

It is not a pristine canyon—the railroad that follows its entire length sees to that—but it is a rugged place with stretches that seem as wild as any of the true wilderness rivers. On the left bank, the river flows along the boundary of the San Isabel National Forest and a Bureau of Land Management Wilderness Study Area known as Aspen Ridge. The wilderness here comes in pieces—places where the tracks bend back from the bank just a bit or a cliff rises high over the river. The wildness here is seen in a set of mule deer tracks leading out to the river from a place under a juniper where the grass of its bed is still flattened, or in the slow circlings of a golden eagle against the sun. It is in a moment, just a moment, when you can look out across the water and not see another boat. In just those moments the Arkansas River can still go wild.

We pull out of the eddy after lunch. From the moment the current catches the boats again, there is almost no time to look around. Once, just above Big Drop, I spot an eagle circling overhead. But before I can point it out, the boat smacks into a rock so big it casts a shadow over almost the whole river and the crew turns back to look at me, silently wondering how I could not see a rock the size of a Mack Truck. "Forward," I yell to get their eyes off me and I don't say anything about the eagle that is already gone anyway.

This is the section of the river that has earned it the reputation as being a carnival ride. There are nearly a dozen separate rapids between lunch and the take-out at Hecla Junction, not including the seven steps of Staircase. It is constant action—Big Drop, Staircase, Widowmaker, Jump Rock, Raft Ripper. All the way down the river I've been worrying about Raft Ripper. Once, in the rain, I hiked upstream from the take-out as far as that rapid and sat watching the pair of sharp rocks in its gut shredding driftlogs. But this time we go through so smoothly and quickly that I have to yell to the boat ahead to ask if that was Raft Ripper.

Graveyard, Last Chance, and we are at the take-out. Stepping from the coolness of the river is like opening a furnace door and so, after the rafts are dried and rolled, I find a patch of shade to sit in while we wait for the shuttle. The river at my feet continues on through Seidel's Suckhole, down through other canyons into the Royal Gorge where even this early in the day the river is likely to be in shadow. Upstream, kayakers are dancing through the rocks of the Numbers Run and some commercial guides are already rigging up for the second of three runs they will make through Browns Canyon today.

It is a busy river. Use has increased 256 percent in the last six years. It is hard to keep a secret these days. The construction of new boat chutes at Buena Vista and Salida may soon connect the separate parts of the river, making it possible for some paddlers to make trips up to four days long on a river that is now used mainly for day trips. The number of people will climb.

The shuttle truck pulls up just as another busload of paddlers drives off. The thought of the number of paddlers carried on the back of the Arkansas River every year makes me suddenly tired. It seems as if the river would wind down like an old clock and stop under all that use. But the memory of the river this morning flowing alone through the ice-blue light comes back to me. Beyond the line of boats waiting to take out, the river is still flowing, curling once around each raft and then just moving on.

3.

THE COLORADO RIVER

PUMPHOUSE RUN

Jeff Rennicke

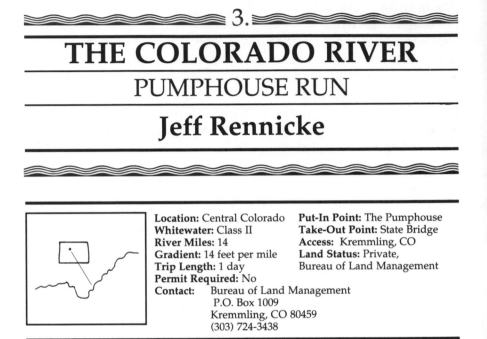

Location: Central Colorado	**Put-In Point:** The Pumphouse
Whitewater: Class II	**Take-Out Point:** State Bridge
River Miles: 14	**Access:** Kremmling, CO
Gradient: 14 feet per mile	**Land Status:** Private,
Trip Length: 1 day	Bureau of Land Management
Permit Required: No	

Contact: Bureau of Land Management
P.O. Box 1009
Kremmling, CO 80459
(303) 724-3438

Up in Rocky Mountain National Park the sun is rising. The first rays of morning spark across the summits of Shipler Mountain, Mount Cumulus and scores of other peaks lighting them like candles. In places outside the deep shadows of the timber, the snow is beginning to melt. The air above the Kawuneeche Valley shimmers with the sound of water, a sound like the tinkling of far-off bells. Streams as clear as the morning ice—Bennett Creek, Big Dutch, Little Dutch, Lost Creek—are humming with the snowmelt. Where the creeks flow together like the strings of some musical instrument there are the star-shaped tracks of ptarmigan in the snow. The tracks mark the beginning of a legend: the Colorado River.

Mountains, deep shadows, ice, ptarmigan, clear water, these are not the images usually brought to mind by the Colorado River. To most people the Colorado River is a river of sandstone canyons and heat, rattlesnakes and water that is usually described as "too thick to drink, too thin to plow." But even legends have to begin somewhere and the Colorado River begins here below the peaks of Rocky Mountain National Park in a series of cold, clear streams small enough to jump over without getting your feet wet. Not far downstream there is a boat launch.

By the time we get to the wide, grassy flat that serves as the put-in point for the Pumphouse Run, we already have the feeling of coming home. Only one of us has ever been here before but that doesn't matter. Add up the days of experience the people we are paddling with have had downstream on the Colorado River and you'd end up with enough days to stretch over the hide of a year. Those days, though, were spent in places where the river comes into its own, canyons with names like Horsethief and Westwater and Cataract and the Grand. It is a little like reading a book backwards, but by coming here to the Pumphouse, the story seems complete. This is the first chapter in the long story of the Colorado River. This is where it all begins.

Our maps, laid out across the hood of the truck and held down by river rocks, call the Pumphouse put-in mile 0. That seems a strange geographic assumption, as if the river flowing past us, almost a stone's throw across, rises out of the ground full-fledged right here beside the truck. It does not.

Just upstream from the put-in, the river emerges from a dark rock slot in the earth known as Gore Canyon. Of all the campfire tales told about the mighty rapids downstream on the Colorado River, what may be the worst of the river's whitewater can be found here before the river even has much of a chance to start. It starts with a bang. Gore Canyon is sliced right through a spur of the Gore Range. In the narrow canyon the river drops up to 100 feet per mile, roaring through rocks as big as a freight train. It is the outer limits of boating on the Colorado River, run by only the very best and then at water levels that put the river at less than full power.

That is upstream. At the Pumphouse the river settles like the waves of a sea after a storm. This is a calm run, Class II, a place to peacefully shake hands with a legend and come to know the Colorado River. More than 40,000 people a year do just that here on the Pumphouse Run. That number makes this the second most popular river in the state next to Browns Canyon on the Arkansas River. Together, Browns Canyon and the Pumphouse account for 75 percent of the commercial river running in the state. To thousands of river runners every year, this is the headwaters of the sport in Colorado.

It is early in the year, before the big run-off and the big crowds, and as we drift away downstream from the put-in there is just one scraggly dog on shore barking and sniffing at our truck tires to see us off. From the start, anyone with Colorado River experience can tell that this is something different, a new angle on an old friend. The road drops quickly from sight although the railroad weaves in and out-of-view on the right bank. The water is clear and cold, more of the mountains than of the desert. The breeze is cool as a drink of water and carries none of the heat that stifles the lower canyons of the Colorado. When the river swings suddenly around a bend, the view carries the snow-capped peaks of the Gore Range instead of sage-brush flats and the shimmer of heat waves.

Still, for all the differences, this is the Colorado River and not far downstream the canyon walls tighten just a bit, forming Little Gore Canyon, and a low growl grows in the throat of the river. The sound, on any part of the Colorado River, is unmistakable: whitewater.

I know it's not some impassable Class VI drop or even one of the gut-tightening falls of Gore Canyon upstream. I've read the guide-books and heard the campfire stories. Still, moving water is a dy-namic platform and there is the element of mystery and fear in en-countering any rapid for the first time. I can't keep my stomach from fluttering a bit as we pull off to the right and climb up on the railroad tracks to get a look.

Needle Eye, it's called. A respectable drop chiseled out of the same dark teeth of rock that shred the river through Gore Canyon upstream and are found at so many of the legendary rapids down-stream, like Skull in Westwater Canyon and Hance in the Grand. If more water were crashing through the rocks here, Needle Eye might inspire some of the same campfire tales. As it is, it is a fun run with just enough waves to splash over the bow of the boat and just enough quick moves to tighten your grip on the oars.

Downstream there are other rapids with poetic names like Screaming Left Turn and The Hole. We stop at each of them to get a look and to take photographs, since few of us have been here before. This is a short run and the photography helps slow us down. And although I don't mention this to anyone in my boat, I don't mind one bit stopping for a quick look before dropping into a rapid that carries a name like Screaming Left Turn.

Despite the names, the whitewater is only Class II, an intro-duction. The holes in the rapids and all the fastwater in-between has me dreaming of being in an open canoe or a kayak. Most of the runs here are done in paddleboats, which get a paddler closer to the river than we can get in our oarboats. Next time.

The walls of Little Gore Canyon fall back a bit as we float past the trickle of water that the map calls Sheephorn Creek and out onto the level ground of Radium Valley. The land softens here. The dark rock that forms rapids like Needle Eye upstream gives way to lighter colors—the green of pasture land, the light brown of grazing cattle, the yellow eyes of a farm cat that jumps straight into the air in surprise as we drift silently around a bend. I tuck the oars under the crook of my knees and lean back, watching a band of clouds drift by like sheep grazing a sky-colored hillside.

It is a mistake. Without warning the bottom of the raft is peeled back like a sardine can. Gone. A patch about exactly the size of a square fire pan is ripped from the bottom of the boat and I am up to my knees in cold water and trying to row the boat that now handles as well as a ring of bologna to the nearest shore.

Unloaded and turned upside-down, the floor of the raft looks like it is equipped with a trap door. A tattered edge on the material looks like it was hooked by a snag of a dead tree sitting just below the surface of the water. It is fixable, just barely, but it will take all the glue, wire and duct tape in the repair kit to do it.

To pass the time while we repair the boat, I tell the story of another victim of this stretch of river: one Captain Samuel Adams.

The year 1869 is well known to any western river runner. That was the year Major John Wesley Powell and his men explored the Colorado River through the Grand Canyon for the first time, filling in one of the last large blank spots on the map of the western United States. That was also the year that Samuel Adams, who called himself "Captain," although his military credentials were less than certain, tried to beat Powell to glory by taking a different route to the Grand Canyon. Instead of going down the Green River from Wyo-ming to the Colorado River and the Grand Canyon, Adams pushed off onto the Blue River on July 12, 1869 with four boats. His aim was to go down the Blue, out onto the Colorado (which was then called the Grand River) and out to California through the Grand Canyon. He never made it.

Adams lost all four boats, built another one, lost that, built another one, suffered the desertion of eight of his 10 men and then, somewhere not far downstream from where we stand repairing our raft, he lost the last of his boats and gave up the voyage. Somewhere far downstream, Powell's group was rowing its way into history. Adams and his last two loyal men gave the river one last look over their shoulders and walked away.

Our boat is fixed. We tip it back upright and set it gingerly in the water. No leaks. We drift off again, back on the water, wounded but still afloat and luckier at least than Samuel Adams.

A band of clouds gathers over the sun like vultures on a kill, and a cold wind comes up. It is early in the rafting season. In a few weeks there will be crowds of rafters in bathing suits having water fights with the bailing buckets, but now as we float alone on the dark water everyone in our two rafts reaches for a sweatshirt at the same time. This is not the desert country of the Colorado. This is the high country and the river carries a chill here it forgets about downstream.

The canyon walls close in again. Red Gorge Canyon. Not far into the clutches of the canyon walls the air echoes again with that familiar ring. Red Gorge Rapid. It seems bigger to me than the ones upstream. Maybe it is just the cold, or the dark sky. Maybe the river is gaining strength, but with the cold seeping into our clothes we don't have time to figure it out and we don't stop to scout. It goes by quickly, as do the others—Red Eye, Yarmony and 360. I am so concerned with keeping the wounded boat off the rocks that could split all the repair work that I hardly notice the cold.

The river has a familiar pull to it now, a deep-muscled strength much like it has downstream, and I feel at home behind the oars. The rapids are not big. The water is still too clear for the name *Colorado*, which is the Spanish word for the color red, and I could probably still throw a rock all the way across the water, but there is no doubt about it now, this is the Colorado River.

Just as the work of keeping the fragile boat off the rocks begins to warm me up, the outline of State Bridge comes into view around the bend, the take-out. I tuck the oars under my knees again and let the boat drift the rest of the way at the pace of the river. In a strange sort of way, with the sections of the river shuffled just a bit, we are living out the dream of Samuel Adams to run the entire Colorado River—Horsethief, Westwater, Cataract, the Grand and now the start of it all, the headwaters run. The circle has been closed. Up in Rocky Mountain National Park, where this circle begins, the sun is slowing going down.

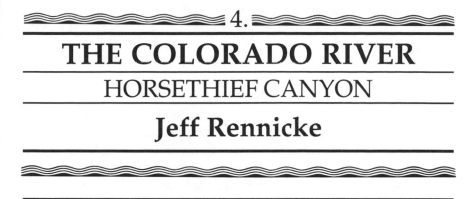

4.

THE COLORADO RIVER

HORSETHIEF CANYON

Jeff Rennicke

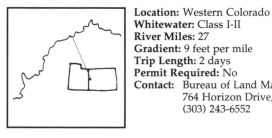

Location: Western Colorado
Whitewater: Class I-II
River Miles: 27
Gradient: 9 feet per mile
Trip Length: 2 days
Permit Required: No
Contact: Bureau of Land Management

Put-In Point: Loma
Take-Out Point: Westwater
Access: Grand Junction, CO
Land Status: BLM, private

764 Horizon Drive, Grand Junction, CO 81506
(303) 243-6552

If there were tracks, they would end at the river. They always do. It's an old trick: make for the river and then head upstream or down. The river won't talk. From this sandy spot along the Colorado River, most have chosen downstream into a series of slickrock canyons that can hide a man from his own shadow. This place has tangled the tracks of a list of horse thieves and outlaws longer than a good hanging rope. It is just the place for people who have a reason not to be found. Even an echo can get lost on its way out. It's that kind of place, a place only desperate people could love—desperate for blue skies to pull down over their eyes like a sombrero, for horizons that could stare down a gunslinger—a desperate place for desperate people, Horsethief Canyon.

Our canoes are lined up on shore like obedient mounts, tethered to a driftlog snubbed in the sand, a "deadman" by local tongue. We too have chosen downstream, the trail of thieves, and we slip out of camp in the half-light of dawn, the mist rising to cover our faces like bandanas, our shadows looking sinister on the water. We are really just a sorry bunch with little to hide, although there is a faint reference in my family tree of a distant relative who was hung as a horse thief. It is enough and the river covers our tracks, leaving us anonymous in the big country that this river wears on its banks like a gunbelt.

There are few places left where a person can vanish like aces from a poker deck—the Maze, Hole-in-the-Wall, Browns Park. Horsethief Canyon is the beginning of that country, if such a country has a beginning. It is a place as big as any in the lower 48 that hasn't been chopped by fences and roads: the last of the wide-open West, pure size. Horsethief Canyon sits in a kind of a saddle. The bone-white Book Cliffs rise 3,500 feet above the river just 50 miles to the north, and the La Sal Mountains of Utah sit snowcapped like a mirage on the horizon, a two-day walk to the southwest. A man can set out walking in about any direction he pleases, go until his boot leather turns to skin and still be a week of Saturday nights from anywhere on the maps.

Even by more conventional means, the size is staggering. We will paddle through two counties that take in more square miles than the state of Massachusetts, yet fewer people live here than in Boulder, Colorado. This is a land of box canyons, wandering echoes, arches cut through solid rock by the wind and pictographs painted on the walls of canyons where the silence is older than the rock.

Only a few hundred yards downstream, beyond a homestead that sits on the north bank surrounded by cottonwoods, the world seems to disappear and there is only canyon. It is good to be out ahead of the heat while the shadows are still a deep shade of purple on the cliffs and the wind is down. The paddling is soft and easy.

This is a canyon that gives you a lot of time to drift, looking for pictographs under the overhangs or wondering at how much the clouds look like lost cattle. One of the first thoughts to cross your mind is how strange it is to find a river here at all in a place where the sun is hotter than a buzzard's breath. Eight inches of rain fell this year, and this year's a wet one. More often, the sky plays cruel games and dangles sheets of rain that dry up just an arm's reach above the desert floor: virga. Some days, when it finally does rain, the slickrock can be so hot that a raindrop can fall, evaporate, rise and condense to fall again farther on. A cruel kind of cat-and-mouse game, but then, the desert can be like that.

That the river is here, though, is no trick of the desert. The mountains far to the east are responsible. Here, the Colorado River is 400 miles from its headwaters in Rocky Mountain National Park and is already a gunshot wide. In the middle of July, the river is still so swollen with run-off and silt that the water sizzles like frying bacon on the bottoms of our aluminum canoes.

Here, the Colorado River is for flatwater paddlers, one of the few places and one of the best that can be run by less-than-expert open canoeists. Twenty-seven miles of river as smooth as slickrock. Horsethief Canyon is not a place for hotdogging; it is back to the basics of canoeing. By the third bend in the river everyone is lying flat as weeds below the highwater mark, no longer even bothering to keep the bows of the canoes straight, letting them drift, dancing with the river, drifting like silver clouds in a sand-colored sky. It is a different feeling from whitewater boating. Once, when the canoes drift close together, we switch boats like outlaws changing horses on the run.

The slow pace makes time seem almost geologic. Time goes as slowly as the river, and gives me a chance to study the rock, looking for the pattern of my fingerprint in the swirls the way some people try to spell out their names in the constellations. The rock along the river is mostly Entrada sandstone, a fancy name for slickrock, as smooth as the flanks of a good horse and the color of bourbon. It is a patient rock and its mood affects the people who come here. Patience, as in the story of the bank-robbing brothers who hit a vault near here and hid out in a cave just downstream for eight days, only to be gunned down as they walked back into the sunshine by a one-man posse who had waited them out.

Only a few miles downriver, not having touched the paddles since the first bend, we pick them up again and paddle hard to catch an eddy at the mouth of a sidecanyon on river left. From the river, Rattlesnake Canyon looks like just another sidecanyon in a landscape fluted with canyons. It is not. Situated 100 air miles from the famous Arches National Park and in the same rock type, the wind and rain have been at work here with the same artistic touches. The result is a geologic treasure chest.

There are arches a coyote would have to crawl through on its belly, others that would scrape the highest branches of the tallest cottonwood and still others large enough to hold a house or, more appropriately, a cathedral. Some say seven arches, some say 13. Once on a solo trip up the canyon, I counted nine. But no matter, Rattlesnake Canyon is Colorado's cathedral in stone.

We stand far below on the canyon floor, our necks bent like bows to stare up at two arches high on the rim. They look like huge blue eyes in the canyon, bridges to somewhere that has been forgotten. On top of a huge spire that lookslike a coiled snake about to strike, there is a flock of pigeons. Their calls fill the canyon with a noise like wind blowing across the top of a bottle.

There is talk about hiking up under the arches. It can be done but it takes some back-tracking and then a long, slow, trailless climb back around to the rim. The heat is up; the air is so hot it stings the nose to breathe it in. Even the ravens have taken to the shadows. July, under a sun as hot as a welder's flame, is not the time for Rattlesnake Canyon. We rest in the scraggly shade of the piñons and then slowly hike back to the river, leaving this place for another day, another story.

Back on the river the edge drops off the heat and there is even a slight breeze. We drift by other sidecanyons—Mee Canyon and others without names—and we are tempted, but the scars of the heat up Rattlesnake Canyon are still deep and make us turn away and stay with the river.

Between the major sidecanyons are countless smaller box canyons, some of them only a dozen yards deep, others going back a bend or two before walling out. These are the canyons that gave this place its name. Rustlers once drove herds of stolen horses down the river in times of low water, using the dead-end canyons as natural corrals that were safe from intrusion when the river came up again. Some say there are still a few strays up there, in the canyons. There are stories of hoofbeats that echo like thunder off hidden walls, and tales of tracks as big as skillets in the mud. It could be, and as we drift by those canyons we listen, but the only sound is the call of a canyon wren like a stone skipping down an empty well.

I keep looking for those tracks each time I pass here. They are some of the faint signs of a human history in this canyon. Once, as a kind of forgotten side trip on the famous Brown-Stanton Expedition of 1889, a man named Frank Kendrick rowed through this canyon in a battered old skiff he bought from the ferry operator at Grand Junction.

The boat he called *Brown Betty*. He hedged on boasting of his trip as a first descent, calling it "the first, on record at least, to successfully navigate, for any considerable distance, the canyons of the [Colorado] River." He had little else to say. In fact, there is little recorded human history here at all—horse thieves rarely leave tracks.

This is a place of natural rather than human history, written in the hieroglyphics of heron tracks in the mud, in the ripples of an ancient wind caught in the sandstone, in the rings of a lightning-struck cottonwood. A trip to Horsethief Canyon is a trip to the old West, older than singing cowboys and pearl-handled six-guns, as old as the river, the rocks and the blue skies.

Evening settles on the canyon like a great bird alighting on the cottonwoods as the sun rides off to the west. Our camp is downstream of Horsethief in a place called Ruby Canyon where the low sun turns the walls the color of a campfire burned low. The railroad tracks come to the river at Salt Creek. Although from most places on the river the tracks are hidden, there is no hiding the howling of the late-night freight, the train stampeding up the canyon like the echo of lost hoofbeats.

It is quiet in the morning, so quiet you can almost hear the sun rise over the canyon walls like the blast of air from a furnace door. Huge boulders of Precambrian schist and gneiss—so old they are barren of fossils—scare the water into a series of boils and choppy waves at a place called Black Rocks. At most water levels it poses no threat to the careful boater, but at high water the hydraulics of the eddies are powerful. These waters have caused more than one death, with the sucking eddies greedily hanging on to the bodies until low water. This time Black Rocks lets us pass without trouble.

We stop at only one place before the take-out, content for most of the day to drift like a raven feather in the wind. It is an unnamed sidecanyon where two simple stick-like pictographs from the Fremont Indians stare out at the river. The pictographs are interesting and echo of a distant time, but I am looking for a legend.

Once, years ago when I first came into this country, an old guide told me of a canyon he had stumbled into while on a solo hike almost half a century before. He was short of food, feverish from drinking brackish water, and, although he'd never admit to it, he was just plain, out-and-out, old-fashioned, you-betcha' honest-to-goodness lost. Crawling down a ledge without ropes, he slipped and fell into a crack below an overhang. When he regained consciousness, he looked up under the overhang and stared into the eyes of an eagle, a pictograph painted golden as if the sun. In all his years in these canyons he'd seen nothing like it and knew it was an important find, but on his way out, disoriented from fever and lack of food, all the canyons seemed to blend into one. Although he has been back to look, he has never found the sun eagle again.

From his description and maps drawn on old scraps of paper, I think that this is the canyon he came down. Each time I float the river I walk up a new ledge as far as I can to look.

I don't find it this trip and maybe it's not there, but the take-out is just downstream, just a clump of cottonwoods and a BLM house-trailer. Like us, some of the horse thieves left the river here. Some went on, like some boaters do, into a canyon called Westwater. We didn't find tracks or hear the hoofbeats of any of the legendary horses of this canyon, although I found a square-nailed hand-forged horseshoe far up one of the canyons and hung it from the bow for good luck. It was enough to make the campfire stories seem real and to make us wonder at the sound of rocks clicking far up the canyons at night. And, though all we have to worry about is one faint reference in a long-ago family tree, we still tread lightly when we step away, leaving only faint tracks that will be gone with the first stirrings of wind. In this country it is best to leave no tracks.

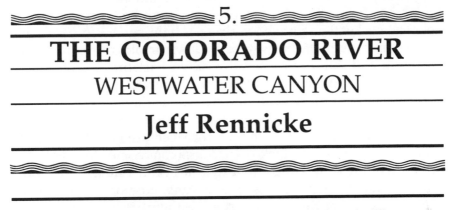

5.

THE COLORADO RIVER

WESTWATER CANYON

Jeff Rennicke

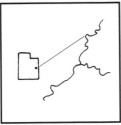

Location: Eastern Utah
Whitewater: Class III–Class IV
River Miles: 18
Gradient: 11.5 feet per mile
Trip Length: 1 to 2 days
Permit Required: Yes
Contact: Bureau of Land Management
P.O. Box M, Moab, UT 84532
(801) 259-6111 ext. 211

Put-In Point: Westwater
Take-Out Point: Cisco
Access: Grand Junction, CO
Land Status: BLM

The bronc riders of the rodeo who follow the circuit have a name for them: the small but powerful horses that can't be figured and can't be ridden the eight seconds before the horn. They call them "stormdogs," rides with the strength of thunder inside them.

Stormdogs. That's the term I am thinking of while I'm lying in the rain on an open beach just upstream from where the Little Dolores River meets the Colorado in Utah's Westwater Canyon. Stormdogs.

Jerry Mallett, old "it-never-rains-in-the-desert" Mallett, is high and dry in the only tent we packed on the trip. Behind me somewhere on the sand is Tom Beck, sound asleep in the four inches of water that have collected in the low spot where he laid his sleeping bag.

Me, I'm not so stoic and pull up a tarp, but there are so many holes in the weary thing that it is like sleeping under a fish net. So I give up the thought of sleep and resign myself to listening to the storm and thinking of the river.

Yesterday, as we floated the flatwater of Horsethief and Ruby canyons upstream, there were no signs of rain and the blue sky rolled off the horizons in every direction. But storms can come up in this country quicker than right hooks in a bar fight. By the time we made camp tonight, with the big water still downstream, the air was thick with rain and thunder rocked the canyon: the river gods rolling bones. Thunder in such a narrow canyon carries all the grace and tune of rolling rocks in an aluminum garbage can.

Between choruses, I hear chunks of the riverbank slumping off into the water. Beyond that, there is the river, just out of sight in the darkness, and flowing thick with debris that comes to it with the storm. Its flow sounds heavy in the dark, carrying as it does the weight of the countless gullies and sidecanyons gone drunk with the rain. In a place like this, the desert edge, there are box canyons and grottos that haven't seen a rain like this in my lifetime.

It is a storm like this that polishes the slickrock. It is a storm like this that lodges the driftlogs high on the ledges like the nests of some long-extinct species of giant bird. It is a storm like this that sets the desert crawling with flashfloods, turning the Colorado River through Westwater Canyon into a bronc on the loose and looking for trouble. A storm like this and the river becomes a stormdog.

Thunder counts the minutes until morning. It is raining so hard that the sun seems to leave a wake as it rises and the best it can do is turn the air a lighter shade of gray. The river has risen and is still rising. The cutbank we scrambled up to tie the boats is underwater; the rafts are scraping on roots that were exposed when parts of the bank collapsed. The biggest change is not in volume but in color. The river is flowing the color of blood. High above the black, inner gorge of Westwater Canyon there is a 1,000-foot cap of sandstone. The claws of the storm have dug deeply into this scarlet rock and the waterfalls pouring over the lip have turned the river the shade of blood.

More than the rain, which is not likely to stop any time soon anyway, it is the look of the river that makes us hesitant to set out. There is an uneasiness in the thick water. Driftlogs appear for a moment at the surface and then are swallowed up again like bones. Snags, fence posts, the spoils of the river's war with its bank, float by as we stand and stare. This day at least, the river is flowing true to its name: red.

Westwater Canyon is one of the fair weather places, normally a reliable early- and late-season run in the West because of the weather. "It never rains in the desert," Jerry Mallett has said on dozens of star-filled nights around campfires in Westwater Canyon. Of the more than 10 trips we can count between us, he has been right. This morning, he is quieter than usual, his cheap raingear already ripped and useless.

As we stand staring at the river, a waterfall appears as if by magic over the cliffs just upstream from camp. Another 30 yards and it would have flushed our porta-potty for us. Coming off the canyon rim, it is even darker than the river, the color of fire. As it weaves toward the river and splashes in, it makes a grating noise, the sound of snakes through wet sand. Then I notice that the noise is everywhere, hanging over the river like smoke. There must be hundreds of these impromptu waterfalls running wild all up and down the canyon, humming in the rain.

Finally, we can't wait any longer. The cold is seeping into our bones and the river is eating away at the spit of beach where we have set up camp. We rig the boats, tying down the best we can with wet ropes over waterlogged gear, and prepare to battle the river. We have three boats, and Jerry, Beck and I have been down the canyon many times. Still, the river is different and all of us sense that, so we talk it over.

Our plan is to stay together, tight, and use signals from boat to boat since scouting will be impossible. There will be no places to land and few, if any, eddies big enough for all three boats. Once we are in the current, we'll have just one chance to get it right.

The moment the boats leave shore, the river jolts us like the first buck of a horse out of the chute, and we use the oars like reins just trying to keep us pointed downriver. The ride begins.

Westwater Canyon is short, only 18 miles, but at its heart is a six-mile stretch that holds 11 major rapids that come in quick succession—Wild Horse, Big Hammer, Marble Canyon, Funnel, Skull, Sock-it-to-me, Bowling Alley, Last Chance. There are no clues to this fury in the Horsethief Canyon section upstream, but just below the start of Westwater Canyon, a dark, shadowless rock rears up out of the ground and clamps the river like the jaws of a trap. It is ancient rock, 1.8 billion years old, twisted, fired, chipped and polished black. It pinches the canyon as narrow as 35 feet in places and, like a rake of the spurs, sets the river wild.

Our three boats have given up trying to stay together as we round the bend into the first rapids. Or rather, where the first of the rapids should be. A river is unpredictable, which is one of the beauties of river running. The high water has washed out Marble and Staircase rapids until there is nothing but a few large waves. But these are only warm-ups. The real heart of the canyon begins at Big Hammer.

Big Hammer has come up with the flood. Huge waves on the right side spin my boat sideways and one of my oars snaps like a twig and is buried by the flood. One of the spare oars is slapped into place just in time to keep us off the wall.

The river picks up speed as it is squeezed by the canyon walls. Funnel Rapid appears through the fog and rain; the high water has made it an enormous pour-over. Beck, in the boat ahead, seems to slip off the edge of the world as the raft slides over the lip and then appears again safe below the drop. As we enter, I see the slot of the drop leads right over a sharp log caught in the rocks and being pummeled by the water. We miss it by pulling left and then turn to signal the third boat, but the fog is too thick. Just at the edge of the drop, the third boat sees the danger and slides left unharmed.

In this stretch of canyon the flood has turned the river into a continuous rapid, no pools, no rests between. The rowing has become a battle.

Then, just above Skull Rapid, the largest and most dangerous whitewater in the canyon, there appears something resembling an eddy on river right. Most of the room is taken up by another of the storm's sudden waterfalls, but there is enough room for the boats. We stop, the boats bouncing against each other and threatening to push each other out of the eddy and back into the current. For the first time we can rest and listen to the river.

It seems to howl. There are falls weeping from nearly every wall in this part of the canyon, some of them big enough, it seems, to kayak through. Even over the sound of the river we can hear the head-sized boulders roll over the falls and smack into the river.

Skull Rapid lies just downstream where the river's course snaps to the left at an odd angle, like a broken bone. The river pours into the wall beyond with such force that it has carved a deep, dark grotto in the canyon wall where the current circles with enough power to catch and hold rafts that stray too far to the right. The boatmen call it the Room of Doom. This eddy was responsible for the naming of

Skull Rapid when a herd of sheep was caught in a flashflood upstream and drowned. For years after that the skulls of the sheep could be seen circling endlessly in the eddy of the Room of Doom.

Rocks are beginning to rain down on us from the waterfall above the eddy, so our decision is made. Beck leads, pulling hard toward the left shore where we may be able to scout the rapid before we run. With the first stroke he knows it is impossible to fight the river. "Go!" he screams over the roar as my boat, still in the main current, passes his. There is really only one way to run Skull Rapid, and scouting it is often done out of sheer respect and a kind of personal offering to the river. I know the route and I set up, pulling downstream and to the left to break the reflection wave and to avoid the immense hole right in the center of the rapid. There is a sudden drop, one I don't recall, and for a sickening moment I wonder if the flood has rolled the rocks in the rapid and changed it, leaving me to run it blind. But then the boat rises over the familiar sidewaves and I spin in anticipation of catching the left edge of the hole.

The wave, usually small this far left, buries us for an instant but then clears, and we are safely into the tailwaves below and in a small eddy waiting for the others. Just before we pull back into the current to continue, I look into the Room of Doom. There, circling in the eddy like the leg bone of some creature, is the oar I shattered upstream.

On the stretch between Skull and the last three smaller rapids downstream, the sky thins and begins to clear. Some of the smaller waterfalls, flowing through draws that have seen nothing but dust and vulture feathers for decades, begin to slacken. The rain has stopped.

Before we get through Last Chance and onto the flatwater stretch before the take-out, the sun has burned the clouds away and the sky looks as if it has never seen a rainstorm. One by one, like the strings of some great instrument, the falls on the cliffs go silent.

Below the rapids we tie the three rafts together to float and lie in the sun to let it warm away the storm. The talk is of whitewater and I think again of rodeos and bronc riders. I notice the river has begun to settle and soften, its color thinning to a lighter brown, chestnut brown, the color of wild horses, the color of stormdogs.

6.

THE COLORADO RIVER

THE GRAND CANYON

Jeff Rennicke

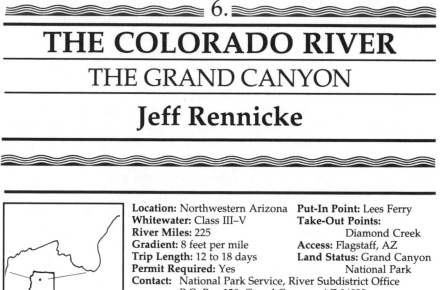

Location: Northwestern Arizona   **Put-In Point:** Lees Ferry
Whitewater: Class III–V   **Take-Out Points:**
River Miles: 225   Diamond Creek
Gradient: 8 feet per mile   **Access:** Flagstaff, AZ
Trip Length: 12 to 18 days   **Land Status:** Grand Canyon
Permit Required: Yes   National Park
Contact: National Park Service, River Subdistrict Office
            P.O. Box 129, Grand Canyon, AZ 86023
            (602) 638-7843

It is late. The air is thick with light, that time of day among these canyons when the sun goes as soft as sand and the river flows the color of gold. The edge has dropped off the heat and shadows have begun to pool on the ledges like dark, clear water. We will camp just downstream, our last camp, around the bend not far, and so we drift.

In my hands, the oars feel as solid as good axe handles, worn to a sheen at the oarlocks by the battles with the rapids upstream— Lava, Crystal, Hermit and the others. But here it is quietwater. Our five boats drift slowly and silently as thought—thoughts of the place we have just come through: the Grand Canyon.

From one of the boats ahead there is laughter, sharp and sounding like the click of pebbles on the cliffs. Nearer, someone is reading from the *Powell Journals* of the first trip through the canyon by river. On this date 114 years ago Major John Wesley Powell and his men were drifting toward their final campsite. With a few burlap sacks of moldy flour but "plenty of coffee," the expedition was drifting out of the "Great Unknown" and into the history books as one of the most daring chapters of western exploration. Powell writes:

> The relief from danger and the joy of success are great. The river rolls by us in silent majesty; the quiet of our camp is sweet; our joy is almost ecstasy. We sit till long after midnight talking of the Grand Canyon. . . .

Our camp at mile 220 is about 50 miles short of where Powell and his men stopped for the night, a section that is now choked with the fat fingers of Lake Mead. That's not all that's different—the pork chops on the grill, the slivers of ice for our whiskey—but the river still rolls by us in silent majesty, the quiet of our camp is just as sweet, and around our campfire too, until long after midnight, the talk will be of these canyons.

To those who have been here, it is *the* canyon and explaining why to someone who hasn't is a little like explaining poetry to a rock. It is simple enough to spout out the statistics: 277 river miles through a canyon that is a mile deep in places and averages nine miles wide (18 miles at the widest), cradling a river that drops 2,200 feet through a hundred rapids, some rated Class V. The experience of the canyon is boxed into a trip which, at 12 to 18 days and up to 30 days off-season, rates as the longest whitewater trip in the lower 48 states.

But numbers no more capture the spirit of the Grand Canyon than the tangle of lines on a topographic map captures the beauty and spirit of Mount Everest. The canyon is too much to be confined that way. Despite the cold whiskey and pork chops, despite Glen Canyon Dam and Hoover Dam, the Grand Canyon has not been totally tamed. It can still be a difficult place. The Colorado is still a cold, powerful river cutting through a landscape of silent rock and heat that can shatter bone. There are rattlesnakes, scorpions, wild box canyons. There are shadows as deep as the river and light that turns to strings of gold at sunset. It is a place where you can feel the claws of thirst ripping at your throat and you can stare at a river full of water a thousand feet below and a day's hike distant. It is a place of elegant contradictions.

Like Lees Ferry, the put-in for a Grand Canyon river trip. Not a ferry anywhere and no one named Lee, it is just a swoop on the topographic maps, a place where the walls of the canyon seem to kneel and allow river runners a place to put their boats in the water. Once, and not so long ago, there was another place to put in up-stream—Glen Canyon—now entombed in the waters of Lake Powell, a strange and somewhat ironic tribute to the man who first pioneered the river. There are people still on the river who remember running "Glen," as they call it. That is an experience that will come again to no one.

In the half-light of half past four in the morning, the cliffs of Lees Ferry are a soft shade of red, and the river, running clear blue, cuts below them and vanishes in the mist. We wake, as usual at most put-in spots, to a chorus of whining air compressors and slamming ammo can lids. For a river put-in, this one is fancy. Still, it is just a gravel beach for rafters going downstream, a concrete pad for the motorized fishermen going upstream, home for a few hopeful ravens, with heat that sticks to you like old grease and a National Park Service employee who sweats on his clipboard while checking permits and safety equipment.

Our group is led by Kim Crumbo, river ranger for Grand Canyon National Park and one of the best and most experienced river runners in the West. Jeff "Rain" Aronson is a professional boatman in the canyon and a wild man who forever looks like he has just stepped off a high wire or blown up a dam. But he is a good rafter and plays a mean mandolin. Of the rest of the boatmen, I have been down the Grand three times; Jerry Mallett is making his second trip in nearly two decades of boating, and Tom Beck, who has run many of the big drops in the West, is making his maiden voyage in the canyon. Few of our 17 passengers have been anywhere near the canyon before and some, like my father, are on their first-ever raft trip. Others, like David Brown and Mimi Wallace, both of Tennessee, are experienced eastern kayakers looking for their first chance at the legendary Grand.

The trip begins slowly the first eight miles. Above that point the river almost always runs clear, too clear for the Colorado, named after the Spanish term for "red." The silt trap of the dam upstream catches the sediment and sometimes the river flows clear the entire length of the canyon. Other times the Paria River, just downstream from the put-in, is enough to mix it up and make the river run its true colors. That first stretch is quietwater, a time to shake out the kinks in your arms and the gear. The boats float under the Navajo Bridge, the last bridge until the Kaibab foot and mule bridge near Phantom Ranch at mile 88.

At mile 8, thoughts of bridges and dams disappear and the first rapid appears. In the canyon's 277 miles, rapids make up only 10 percent of the horizontal distance, much less than it might seem from the canyon's reputation as one of the foremost whitewater stretches on the continent. But again the numbers are deceiving. Those hundred rapids make up more than 50 percent of the vertical fall and include a list of big drops like Hance, Hermit, Granite, Crystal and the legendary Lava. Then there are the others, like Badger Creek Rapid at mile 8.

It is a classic V-shaped drop with a tongue as wide and smooth as a new stretch of highway. In its heart there is a single, lovely wave that reaches out and tosses the boat like a bubble on a breeze. The fact that it is the first in the canyon makes it all the more sweet.

Soap Creek Rapid, the tail end of the one-two punch, is as different from Badger as sunshine is from storm clouds. By Soap Creek the river has gone dark and muddy, the "too thick to drink, too thin to plow" consistency that the river is noted for. The color and the unruly waves make it difficult water to read and the pattern is as erratic as a bucking horse. The chop keeps the oars from getting a good, clean bite. It is one of those rapids that looks best from downstream, looking over your shoulder.

The first day of a Grand Canyon trip is usually short, a taste, and that is enough. We camp just downstream from Soap Creek. Camps in the Grand Canyon are as river camps should be: sand, a roof of stars, a cool breeze wafting up the canyon after a hot day, the sounds of the river harmonizing with Rain's mandolin. Despite high use, the camps are clean, because of the strict regulations of the National Park Service and the respect for the canyon shown by most boaters. Tents are rarely needed, and even then are more for privacy and protection from the sun than against the rain.

Tonight it is calm and starry. I pick a spot along the ledge near the river to lay my sleeping bag. The water is running high—40,000 cubic feet per second—and the tone of the river is deep and heavy. A river, any river, carries with it sounds not unlike music and a wild river's tone is always the sweetest. The Colorado River is no longer wild—a string of dams up and down its length has seen to that, and its music has changed. But it has not stopped, and it is good to lie back and listen to the river dreaming of wilder days. Even dams can't last forever and the river always flows.

Mornings begin with a ritual—the quiet clank of pots at the kitchen set-up and the first reluctant hisses of the campstoves. At the first hint of dawn, Randy Udall, one of the hard-barked kayakers, is up brewing the first pot of coffee. (Kayakers are always the first ones up.) It will be the fourth pot before everyone is up and the sixth before we are on the river.

It is the Roaring Twenties today, a series of rapids between mile 24 and mile 29. At this water level most are just straight shooters, though at times they can be more. When the water slows, we are at Silver Grotto for lunch.

The grotto is one of the most magical spots in the canyon, a place where the false red sheen of the Redwall limestone, stained the color of blood by the Supai and Hermit formations above, has gone and the rock shows its true silver colors. Once, on another trip long ago, we stood at Silver Grotto and watched a full moon rise behind, for a moment lighting a spot on the wall across the river in the shape of an hourglass, like a beam of light in an ancient temple. It seemed like things were in line that night, things bigger than us that we did not control. When we looked again, the light had faded.

Today there is sunshine, but the rocks are still slick, worn smooth by the floodwaters that sometimes run here. Still, even in broad daylight, it is impossible not to see in the pale silver rocks of the grotto a light the color of moon.

Below, there is another of the canyon's long, quiet stretches where the river snakes by the emerald falls of Vasey's Paradise and the deep amphitheater of Redwall Cavern. With the oars out of the water and our feet up, we lie back and watch the canyon walls. This is the way to see the Grand Canyon, one bend at a time, one wall to study before moving on to the next. This way the canyon reveals itself slowly, enticingly. Like a fan dancer it is not meant to be seen all at once the way it is by buzzards or the fly-over tourists from Vegas. Our culture has tried to package the landscape into neat bundles that can fit on postcards and be sold as scenery, but the Grand Canyon doesn't fit on postcards or into the viewfinders of instamatic cameras. Time is as much a part of the experience as whitewater.

In the canyon, time is measured in two ways. First, there is the time on the quietwater to let the colors of the canyon soak in: the light brown of the shales like fine leather, and the red, cinnamon red, of the limestones. Then there is the geologic time shown in the rock behind the colors. Floating just below Redwall Cavern with all the boats together, Crumbo talks about the rocks and the 330 million years, the ancient dance of oceans and deserts that turned to stone. "It makes our 70 years here on earth seem insignificant, doesn't it," my father asks. "Or precious," Crumbo says, looking at the chalky outline of a fossil embedded in the canyon wall.

After days in the Redwall formations of Marble Canyon, the horizons open up for a time near Nankoweap Rapid, showing more sky and longer views. From near Tanner Canyon the South Rim is visible and the sight is comforting after so many days in a tight canyon. Because of the shape of the canyon, there are few places where the rim is visible from the river or, for that matter, places where the river is visible from the rim. But for the few miles in this stretch of river, the canyon is open, airy and inviting.

It is here that the most concentrated evidence is found of the early inhabitants of the canyon. At Nankoweap the walls have eyes in the ruins of the ancient dwellings set up in the cliffs. At Unkar Delta the ground is littered with potsherds, the ceramic footprints of the Anasazi, a Navajo term for "the Ancient Ones," who lived in the canyon area for hundreds of years with populations as high as several hundred. Then, around 1150 A.D., they vanished. These few potsherds, the ruins and a few stick figurines as fragile as dust, are some of the only clues to a civilization and a view of the world from life in the canyon. A clue, at least, to the Anasazi's sense of beauty is that they chose to settle on the Unkar Delta.

The openness of the canyon is short lived. Near mile 77 another rock rears its head, black as a starless sky and as hard as time. Vishnu schist forms the walls of the Upper Granite Gorge in the canyon; it is the oldest rock, the basement, and is so dark it seems to swallow the light. The air seems cooler here, the shadows bottomless. It is no mistake that the biggest rapids in the canyon appear in the hardest rock formation.

We stop to scout Hance Rapid and then run without mishap. Sockdolager comes up quickly but looks not quite so bad and so we run without scouting. There, in its gut, is a hole shaped like a claw that seems to draw the whole river toward it. The run is not so difficult really, just a hard pull to the left.

I don't pull hard enough. The light boat does not break the reflecting wave and we are thrown back into the hole. There is the sensation of speed, a shadow and then all goes dark. We are in the water, beneath the upside-down boat. Gear is hitting me in the head and face and there is a sound like mountains moving. Finally, the light grows brighter and I come up just upstream of the boat, grab the flip line and crawl on top. Within seconds everyone who was in the raft is safely on top, and with the line we right the boat and I'm back behind the oars, rowing. The only losses are a pair of sunglasses and some pride.

Camp is just above Grapevine Rapid and the solid ground feels good beneath my feet. But the wind switches in the night, and all through my sleep I hear the rumbling of Grapevine just below.

River running is akin to rodeo riding and when you've flipped you get right back on the horse. We run Grapevine smoothly. I am back in the saddle after my first flip. Around the fire later, Crumbo puts his arm around me and says, "There are just two kinds of boatmen: those who have flipped and those who are going to." Maybe it's the words, maybe it's just the whiskey and the warm fire, but the flip seems behind me now, a long way.

Phantom Ranch marks a change in the trip. Not only are there the bridge and the new passengers who hiked down the Bright Angel Trail, but the inner gorge squeezes even tighter here creating a quick succession of rapids: Horn Creek, Granite, Hermit . . . and then Crystal.

Lava is the legend but Crystal is the rapid most boatmen think about the hardest. The nervousness gets as thick as river coffee the morning before Crystal and the good ones know just how to break it. Aronson appears just after breakfast wearing a black slip, a garter belt, well-placed padding, ruby lipstick and a lacy, black bonnet over his bald and sunburnt scalp. Without a word he mounts the bow of a raft as his stage, cocks an arm behind him in parody of the one-armed Major Powell and quotes from the journals in his best baritone:

We are now ready to start our way down the Great Unknown. . . . What falls there are, we know not; what rocks
beset the channel, we know not; what walls rise over the
river, we know not. Ah well, we may conjecture many things.
The men talk cheerfully as ever; . . . but to me, the cheer is
somber and the jests are ghastly.

Shouting the final words, Aronson snaps the book shut with a bang, and with a purse of his ruby red lips already running in the heat, stalks off across the sand, his garter belt slipping down around his ankles. The tension is broken.

At least until the pool above the rapid. Major rapids like Crystal constrict the river channel so tightly that the water goes almost dead above, as if even it is nervous about what lies ahead. The stillness makes for an agonizingly slow approach.

Until the evening of December 7, 1966, Crystal was a minor rapid. A storm tossing 14 inches of rain on the bare bones of the sidecanyon created a flash flood that spewed house-sized boulders into the river's path, creating a rapid that today will shiver the timbers of anyone who runs it. A right-hand bend with a tongue of fast water grabs with unexpected power and aims the boat toward a pair of deep holes, breaks inward and forms a kind of gunsight passage. But the real creature of Crystal is the one huge, exploding hole smack in the middle of the river that can shake the rocks on the opposite shore when it breaks.

Dories have flipped here, rafts and j-rigs have flipped, even the 37-foot motor rigs have been tossed end-for-end. Crystal is not to be fooled with and even those boatmen who have rowed it a hundred times approach it humbly each new time.

At this high water level, we scout for nearly an hour, debate a portage and then decide on a run minus most of the passengers. The runs are not pretty, but soon all five of the boats are safely below and the crew is re-loaded. There is little talking until the roar of Crystal Rapid fades slowly as we drift downstream.

With Crystal behind, the river turns to gems: Sapphire, Turquoise and Ruby rapids all in a stretch of less than four miles. Rapids like Tuna Creek, Serpentine, Dubendorf and Upset: this is the whitewater action the canyon is noted for, the times in the spray.

Here too are the mysterious sidecanyons of the Grand. Slicing down from the South Rim are Elves Chasm with its stair-stepped falls and monkeyflowers, the narrow serpentine passages of Matkatamiba and the blue-green Shangri-la of Havasu. These are just the popular ones, the tourist routes. There are others, like Fossil Canyon, where a wide and airy walk turns into a crawl between walls 500 feet high and six feet apart, or the mouth of Galloway Canyon with Aronson standing on his head at the lip of a 1,000-foot drop, legs wobbling in the wind. There is a waterfall lined with columbine in Stone

Canyon, and places so quiet you can hear your own heartbeat.

On the still water above Lava Falls you can sometimes hear your heartbeat too. As with all big rapids, the approach to Lava is slow and you are forced to stare into the black eyes of the lava formations that line the river here. At a column of lava called Vulcan's Anvil a mile above the falls, the tradition is to toss coins on the rock to appease the river gods. "Do you suppose they would take a check?" someone asks, trying to break the tension. No one laughs loudly.

There are scouting locations on both sides of the river above the drop. At this water level we choose the left, and stand on a high ridge 10 feet above the river. Still the waves look huge. Lava Falls is called "the most exciting 12 seconds of your life" by the boatmen.

Lava has a way of destroying even the best laid plans. Besides, as Crumbo poetically puts it, "the more complicated the plan, the more complete the mayhem." So we choose a simple and straight left-side run away from the famous bubble line that leads into the huge hole. Still, it is Lava Falls and Lava is the legend. It is the summit of whitewater and, as climbers know, there is nothing quite like the summit.

Our runs are smooth, the waves cresting and laying down just in front of our rafts. In the midst of Lava Falls, the campfire stories you have been hearing all your life suddenly seem to ring with truth— tales of a boat flipped twice by successive waves that ended upright and dry in an eddy below, tales of dories spun atop a wave like a toy. "That was the most exciting thing in my life," my father says to me after the run, "since I met your mother." Everything said about Lava seems true, and even if it is not, it probably could be.

There is a feeling that a canyon trip begins and ends at Lava Falls. That is a sadly narrow view of this place, a bumper sticker attitude. There are still 55 to 60 miles of river downstream before the waters of Lake Mead still its heart. It is time to trade stories of Lava, watch the sun like diamonds on the water, bounce through rapids like 205 and 217. It is time to work on stories for the final campsite.

Our fire is dying down and most of the crew have already gone off to bed. The boatmen are the only ones still left, still awake, thinking maybe if they just stay awake the trip won't really end tomorrow. For a time it is quiet. Aronson picks his mandolin and then someone reads the last passage from Powell's journals by the faint firelight:

You cannot see the Grand Canyon in one view, as if it were a changeless spectacle from which a curtain might be lifted, but to see it you have to toil ... but if strength and courage be sufficient for the task . . . a concept of sublimity can be obtained never again to be equaled on the hither side of Paradise.

Each trip is only one view, a glimpse really. I think back to all the sidecanyons we drifted by without stopping to hike up. What falls were there, what play of shadow and light? The canyon comes with a price, even today. It may no longer be the moldy flour and hardships that Powell and his men faced, but even now the canyon is too big for a single lifetime and the price is in the recognition of that fact. Then too, there are upstream winds, rattlesnakes, the likes of Crystal and Lava. But no one said it would be easy. The Grand Canyon is a difficult place. The good things rarely come easy, the great ones never do.

To the soft voices and the music of the river and the mandolin, I doze off. When I wake up, the moon has risen, the fire is cold and the boatmen have all crawled off. The only sound is the river flowing, always the river flowing.

7

DESCHUTES RIVER

LOWER CANYON

Brian Clark

Location: North Central Oregon   **Access:**   Maupin, OR
Whitewater: Class II-III   Bend, OR
River Miles: 42   **Land Status:** Indian
Gradient: 13 feet per mile   Reservation,
Trip Length: 3 days   BLM, city, private
Permit Required: Yes
Contact: Oregon State Parks
            525 Trade Street SE, Suite 301, Salem, OR 97310
Put-In Point: Trout Creek Flat
Take-Out Point: Sherar's Falls

They don't call the Deschutes River one of Oregon's top trout streams without good reason. It's not unusual for an experienced fly-fisherman to land a half-dozen redsides, as rainbow trout are called around here, in an hour or two of angling.

But the Deschutes is more than just a fishing river. Coursing north toward the Columbia River on the east side of the Cascade Range in the center of the state, this premier trout stream is also a great novice and family whitewater adventure. It is one of the more heavily boated rivers in Oregon, and offers single- and multi-day trips in rafts and inflatable kayaks that provide a delightful introduction to Class II and Class III rapids.

A designated state Scenic Waterway, the Deschutes River is also a lesson in contrasts. The clear, cold blue-green waters of the river— that make it a quality trout habitat—ramble through the high desert.

It is a flowing oasis that cuts a green swath through brown cliffs, basaltic columns, dry grasslands and hills that look as if they have not seen rain in months. In the summer, that's generally true. Though the Deschutes possesses more hydroelectric potential than any other Oregon river, its lower 100 miles remain free-flowing. At the Trout Creek campsite, a sign bears the words of former Secretary of the Interior Stewart Udall: "Future generations will remember us for the roads we don't build." In this case, roads would be dams.

Three of the Cascade Range's biggest volcanos are near the river, and lava from them and other eruptions buried the land under thousands of feet of flows in the past 20 million years. The Deschutes Canyon itself is a relative newcomer in geologic terms. Several hundred feet deep in spots, it was scoured out by glaciers and by the floods that were created when the big melt occurred only a few thousand years ago. It was named by French Hudson Bay Company trappers for its waterfalls, which are now buried under a reservoir at the river's confluence with the Columbia. Originally known by its Indian name, *Towornehiooks*, the Deschutes was once also called Clark's River, for William Clark of Lewis and Clark fame.

An occasional abandoned shepherd's cabin can be found along the banks, and a few cattle are still raised in the hills above the Deschutes. As in other locales, sheep and cattle didn't mix well here and once caused violent range wars between cattlemen and sheep ranchers. At one point, more than 2,400 sheep were slain in an attempt by the cattlemen to scare the sheep ranchers out. The canyon was also the site of a vicious battle between two rival railroad companies that built competing lines on either side of the river.

These days, instead of finding shepherd or cowboy cabins, you are likely to find modern—even posh—versions of fishermen's cabins along the river, because among fly-fishermen, owning a cabin on this stream is like owning a bit of heaven. Not just trout are caught here; whitefish, steelheads and Chinook salmon are also taken.

My family's three-day trip down the Deschutes began at the appropriately named Trout Springs, some 35 miles south of the railroad town of Maupin. We drove from the Maupin campground through the high desert, dropped down into the canyon upstream and came to a park area with lovely green grass—a rare commodity in this neck of the woods. We were greeted at the put-in by Mike Burns and Craig Hamilton, the amiable boatmen who were to be our raft guides on the 42-mile sojourn.

Suntan lotion slathered on and my kayak unloaded from the top of the shuttle van, we pushed off from the bank and immediately felt the river's pull. Flowing at 5,000 cubic feet per second, the Deschutes runs swiftly all summer long. And while it does not scare experienced boaters, it is a powerful, pushy river not to be taken lightly. More than once I shook my head when I saw rafters running its rapids without wearing life jackets and often with a beer in one hand.

Loading up the drybags that held our clothes and camping gear, I had worked up a small sweat, so I plopped over and did a quick Eskimo roll in my kayak to cool off. I shivered as I came up. The water felt as if it thought it were still snow somewhere high in the Cascade Range west of Bend, where the Deschutes' headwaters can be found in Lava Lake near South Sister Peak.

Beside me, my wife Shelley paddled an inflatable kayak, which is a fun way to learn about one-person boats and how they handle in eddies, currents and rapids. The next step up is a hard-shelled kayak. We floated downstream while Mike rowed the gear boat and Craig guided the passenger raft that carried our 15-year-old son, Nathaniel. It was his first time rafting and his eyes were wide with anticipation, taking in everything around him. But he wasn't a novice to streams, for he'd spent a good portion of his young life searching for trout in creeks and freshets in the California Sierras near our home. It hadn't taken any arm twisting to get him to come on the Deschutes.

Trout Creek Rapid was a gentle riffle, the kind that makes a raft bounce and flex a bit. A mile downstream came the Warm Springs River, which flows out of the Indian reservation that bears its name. It is home to remnants of the Walla Walla, Wacos and Paiute tribes. It looked dry and desolate. Typical, I thought, of the kind of land Native Americans were allocated after they were overwhelmed by the movement of whites across the continent in the last century. It seemed sadly appropriate that the town of Maupin was named for the man who killed Snake Chief Paulina in 1866. Ironically—or perhaps out of respect for his fighting skill and his refusal to surrender and live on a reservation—a mountain, lake, creek and town all bear "Bullet Proof" Paulina's name.

Skookum Creek and Oak Creek came next, and then White Horse Rapid, which dropped 25 feet in the first 300 yards and was the first rapid of significance on our run. We all chose to run the rapid on the right, avoiding some of the holes and punching through others with spray splashing over the front of our boats.

Lunch came on a cool bank beneath a spreading oak tree. Though I'd been wearing polypropylene under my paddling jacket, and though it was warm outside, the cold water had chilled me to the core. While my family sought shelter from the sun under a tree, I basked under ol' sol trying to get some heat back into my bones. It helped to get a sandwich or two into my gullet.

A few more minor rapids followed lunch and Craig let Nathaniel try his hand at rowing. It was a great idea. Nathaniel had been in something of a teenage funk the week before, speaking in monosyllables with a minimum of animation. On the route north from California, he'd driven some. Not only did he frighten us a time or two, he'd gotten frustrated with our back-seat driving.

Now, though, he was away from his parents in a boat with a couple of rugged young guides who would inspire any teenager. And not only were they friendly to him and not doing dumb things like telling him to take out the garbage, they were actually letting him row a big raft. He was in heaven as they floated down the river, talking of skiing in Utah, skateboarding, riding mountain bikes and fishing for trout. Nathaniel cut his river eyeteeth on drops that were big enough to make things interesting but offered no danger. In fact, some of the companies that operate on the Deschutes offer "row-your-own" boats that the passengers get to guide themselves downstream through the rapids. A head guide comes along in his own boat to give instructions.

Camp came on a big bend across the river from a jumble of basalt columns that had been twisted and laid flat over on themselves. Beneath the pillars were several big eddies, perfectly suited for a novice to practice eddy turns. Shelley and I switched boats. She timidly entered the main current and tried to execute a ferry across the river in my hard plastic kayak, a Perception Dancer that had seen more than a few years of kayak wars on California rivers.

Quicker than you could say "boo," she was upside-down, the current having caught the upstream edge of her kayak when she leaned into the current—violating one of the cardinal rules of kayaking.

A few minutes later we were on the opposite shore, warming up and going over the technique for leaning downstream so that the river pushes against the flat bottom of the kayak instead of catching the upstream edge. Shelley shook out her willies and climbed back into the kayak. She paddled to the point just in back of where the eddy met the main current, sucked in a breath to help screw up her courage, drove the boat out in the current and, with a few crisp strokes, ferried across the river like a pro. On the other side, she exhaled a big breath of air and grinned.

Back at camp, Nathaniel was nowhere to be found. He'd headed for some small riffles and pools upstream to try his hand with a couple of flies he'd bought at a Maupin fly-fishing store. He'd also gotten some expert advice from Mike, an avid fly-fisherman who had run the Deschutes at least 30 times. An hour later Nathaniel was back with two trout—a perfect addition to our dinner. That night we sat around the fire under the tall ponderosa pines, picking the white and pink meat off the trout and watching the moon rise over the Mutton Range. In the distance, we heard animals scuffling and wondered if they were bobcats, mountain lions or mule deer that call the canyon home.

The next morning, we explored caves above the campground before heading downstream toward Buckskin Mary Rapid just below Eagle Creek. We caught the green tongue in the middle of the rapid and bounced down the roller-coaster standing waves to the bottom of the drop. Above us, red-tailed hawks circled looking for food. Mergansers floated beside us on part of the trip and we saw the jug-like mud nests of countless cliff swallows on the canyon walls.

At the northern end of the Indian reservation we crossed the Power Boat Deadline, which meant boats with engines could cruise the river for fish below that point. While I am not crazy about sharing whitewater rivers with power boats, the dozen or so we encountered the next few days weren't overly loud or obnoxious. Fortunately, they weren't big jetboats.

That night Nathaniel hit the big time with his fishing, landing another seven trout, all but one of which he released. Rain fell and the wind blew at our camp near the Oregon Trunk Railroad tracks. A train even rumbled by. But we didn't mind one bit. We were dry inside our tents as we slept beside the growling river.

The next morning Nathaniel used the early hours to his best advantage and caught even more trout. It made for a great breakfast. And things got even better, for the best rapids of the trip were right around the corner. They included Wapinitia and Boxcar Rapid—the latter named for a big train wreck in 1954 that claimed the lives of the brakeman and the engineer. We ran Boxcar on the left, sliding past a pour-over below a ledge and skirting a hole below an underwater boulder. It was a bouncy ride and I paddled my kayak back upstream a few times to blast through the hole again and again. For the next two miles, we lay back in our boats and watched salvos of water being fired from buckets in the mini-war between an armada of six rafts just ahead. Twenty minutes later we were in Maupin and ready for lunch.

Bellies full, we paddled on to Surfers Alley where kayakers often hang out to play in the series of waves. Then it was Oaksprings Rapid, split by an island and next to a fish hatchery. Mike rowed his boat close to the inside of the island, missing the hole at the bottom and sliding over a series of sharp ledges below. No place to take a tumble, Mike said, for more than a few shins and knees have been skinned on the serrated ledges below the main drop. I took it on the far left, caught a small hole for a few seconds and then let my kayak bounce happily downstream through a series of small reversals.

From there on we basked in the sun, ran a few more small rapids and made sure we beached our boats at the take-out above Sherar's Falls—an unrunnable 15-foot cascade that looked as if it would easily drown anyone foolish enough to attempt it. Amazingly, Mike told us, it's not unusual for a boat or two of somewhat inebriated rafters to miss the take-out and float into the jaws of Sherar's Falls. And, with the luck that drunks often seem to possess, they float out at the bottom, still breathing and not much worse for the wear.

An hour later, we said our good-byes to the guides as they headed off to meet another rafting group. When we hopped in our car for the drive home, I was wishing that our trip was starting over and that I knew a little more—no, make that a lot more—about fly-fishing.

8.

THE DOLORES RIVER

DOLORES CANYON/ SLICKROCK CANYON

Jeff Rennicke

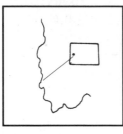

Location: Southwestern Colorado **Put-In Point:**
Whitewater: Class III–Class IV   Bradfield Ranch
River Miles: 98   **Take-Out Point:** Bedrock
Gradient: 15 feet per mile   **Access:**   Telluride, CO
Trip Length: 5 days   Cortez, CO
Permit Required: No   **Land Status:** BLM
Contact: Bureau of Land Management, Hwy 550 S
             P.O. Box 1269
             Montrose, CO 81401
             (303) 249-7791

The late afternoon light at Five Pines camp is the color of stained glass. The low sun reflects off the canyon walls and filters down through the branches of the ponderosa pines in strands like spun glass. It gives the campsite the solemnness of a cathedral.

It is a fitting feeling on a river with such a long, pious name as El Rio de Nuestra Señora de Dolores. When the men of the Dominguez/Escalante Expedition named it in 1776, it probably seemed too wild and high-spirited a river to be burdened with such a weighty title. But sometime in the spring of 1984, 108 years later, the River of Our Lady of Sorrows, what we now call the Dolores, began carrying all the sadness of its name.

This is not our first trip on the Dolores and it won't be our last. But it is the one we'll always remember and talk about around the campfire. Twenty miles upstream from our campsite the gates of the $452 million McPhee Dam will soon be wrenched shut, taming the wild river. Many of the people who fought the project for years—Jerry Mallett of the Western River Guides Association, Sally Ranney of the American Wilderness Alliance, Tom Beck, Bill Dvorak and others—have come here to pay tribute to the river in the only way they know how: by paddling it.

A party of kayakers including Mark Udall of Colorado Outward Bound, Maggie Fox of the Sierra Club and Ted Kerasote who has written of the river's plight, float by our camp. Mark paddles over to us as the others float by. For a long time, he sits in his kayak staring upstream and talking about the dam before paddling on alone, looking small against the river.

The 275-foot dam will not kill the river. In fact, if the Bureau of Reclamation, which runs the dam, will cooperate, a release pattern could be worked out that would moderate flows and actually extend the paddling season on a river known for its erratic flows. But it will not be the same; the river will have lost a part of its heart. Some of the last free-flowing water, a little piece of history, is flowing by our campsite tonight. I sit on the rocks in the fading light until it is too dark to see, watching.

The Dolores River begins, like so many rivers of the southern Rockies, in the melting snows of the San Juan Mountains. Flowing off of Lizard Head Pass outside of Telluride, the Dolores begins as a clear mountain stream headed south toward the San Juan River, but somewhere around the town of Dolores, the river changes both its course and its temperament. It turns north to become a tributary of the Colorado River and it leaves the mountains for the first of its desert canyons.

The canyons echo with history. First came the hoofbeats of Butch Cassidy and his Wild Bunch, who robbed the San Miguel Valley Bank in Telluride on June 24, 1889, to the tune of $10,500, then used the maze of the river's canyons to mask their getaway. Next came the ring of picks and shovels as a string of mining booms—silver, carnotite, vanadium and a list of other mispronounceable minerals—sparked dreams of riches. But every boom was met with a bust and the dreams did not pan out. More than a hundred miles of the

Dolores' course have been studied and recommended for inclusion in the National Wild and Scenic Rivers System, but just as with its dreams of mining glory, the protection has not yet come. Now the river flows alone.

Alone except for the paddlers. We push off into the current early, surprisingly early for a party as big as ours—four rafts and several kayaks—considering how late we stayed up watching the starlight between the branches of the pines. Sunlight replaces starlight as we float through the upper part of the Dolores Canyon known as Ponderosa Gorge. It is a strangely beautiful mix of desert canyons and pine trees that soften the edges of the cliffs.

The river is flowing strong, around 4,000 cubic feet per second; the pace of the river is straight and fast. Canyon walls flip faster than the guidebook pages. The rapids begin where the river's course grows indecisive. At Glade Canyon the river loops like a paper clip, first northeast, then swinging southwest, then northeast again, picking up speed. In the upper stretches the river drops at twice the rate of the lower canyons, making the low gradient figures deceiving. Here, the Dolores runs hard—Glade Rapid, Molar, Canine.

In the bow of my raft, Congressman Tim Wirth and Kevin Klose, a writer for the *Washington Post*, look puzzled as I slide the boat to shore at a calm stretch. "Just listen," I say in answer to their looks. Just downstream there is a rumbling. Kevin describes it as "a dragon crooning." I don't know; I've never heard a crooning dragon. But then again, I know what is making the noise: Snaggletooth Rapid.

It is named for the one fang-like rock that seems to shear the river at the bottom of the rapid. A long series of jagged waves upstream seems to draw the entire force of the river into the tooth rock to be shredded. A well-worn portage trail along the left bank is a tribute to the size and power of the rapid. Many kayakers and even rafters take what has become known as the "shoulder run" by putting their boats up on their shoulders and carrying them along the bank.

Going around the rapids has a long history. Even Otis "Doc" Marston, who named the rapid on the first recorded trip down the Dolores in 1948, lined his boat, three passengers and a black dog named "Ditty" around Old Snaggletooth. "A rapid-happy riverman," could run Snaggletooth, said Marston, "but he would need to be very happy."

We're feeling happy and are not burdened by the heavy wooden boat that Marston was rowing nor any dogs named "Ditty." In the heat of high noon, the day seems to stand still as we stare at the river. We decide to run it. It may be our last chance at Snaggletooth while the river is still wild.

From the oars of the second boat, I watch the first disappear into the first wave. We follow. Worrying about the tooth rock, the paddlers overlook the power of the waves. We hit them straight on and water crashes into the raft, filling us up and making the boat sluggish. Still, we have read the rapid right. I am set up on the right line and the raft slips by the tooth, where the water broken by the rock makes a hiss, a noise like a sharp knife cutting the air.

Then we are past but the boat is so full of water that I can't make the eddy and we are swept downstream into the long stretch of Class III water below. With hundreds of pounds of water in the boat, it is like rowing a rock. We careen off a log jam at the tip of the island, and lose an oar. Kevin and Tim are bailing so hard I can hardly see through the spray. It is a half-mile or more before I can catch an eddy. The others float by safely through Snaggletooth, and we follow behind, bouncing off the undercut canyon at a rapid known poetically as The Wall. Finally we pull off for lunch and lie in the sun, glad to be on solid ground.

With the big drop at Snaggletooth behind us and a long Class III rapid below known as Mile Long, the river comes out of the high land of ponderosa pines, losing its mountain touches. Here it flows into a harsher place where the shadows are sharper and the light is as clear as broken glass. The river changes too, opening onto a wide flat at Slickrock where there is a small store with ice cream, water for 10 Cents a Gallon and a *Return of the Mutants* comic book that will supplement our river library nicely. While we haul the heavy water jugs back to the river, a trio of ravens is circling the canyon downstream, so high they look like windblown ashes.

Just below the ravens the river drops back into a canyon—Little Glen Canyon—named after the place now drowned by the waters of Lake Powell behind the Glen Canyon Dam. The irony is poetic: one canyon drowned by a dam, another that could be dried up. Drifting on the quietwater, I can hear someone up ahead talking about the high-quality trout fishery that will be created in the tailwaters of the McPhee Dam. And it's true; the Dolores could become one of the best float-fishing trips in the Southwest. River otter are being introduced. The changes coming with the closing of the dam upstream will not be as drastic as the drowning of Glen Canyon when that dam closed on the Colorado River. But the place will be different somehow and we can feel it as we drift through the five miles of Little Glen Canyon.

The canyon gives way to Big Gypsum Valley, a wide expanse just long enough to make entering the narrow Slickrock Canyon like passing through a keyhole. The sun rarely finds the bottom of the slickrock, and we row in shadows between walls even tighter and narrower than the upstream canyons. The narrowness of the canyon makes it seem like it should be echoing with the thunder of huge rapids, and there are some good Class III runs. Bull Canyon Rapid can be challenging at high water, but for the most part the river winds contentedly, almost tying itself in a knot at a place called The Cloverleaf. The river seems hesitant to leave the canyon.

And so are we. We get a late start the next morning after camping at Coyote Wash, having stayed long around the campfire trading stories. It is our last camp on the trip. The river continues another 76 miles from where we will take out through Paradox Valley, through long and winding Mesa Canyon into Gateway Canyon, then into Utah and through the other legendary rapid of the river called Stateline before flowing into the Colorado River.

Mesa Canyon is on my mind as the boats drift the last miles of the trip. One of the stories around the campfire last night told of a 4-by-6-foot wooden flume strung 400 feet above the river in the canyon. It was the scheme of the owners of the Lone Tree Placer Mine to construct it. The cliff walls were loaded with gold, or so the engineers thought. The water needed to sluice the gold, however, was 400 feet below in the river. So, a string of workers, perched along a wooden platform suspended from the sheer cliff face, set thousands of brackets one by one to secure the flume.

It was an epic construction job requiring 1.8 million board-feet of lumber and almost costing the life of one of the workers who slipped from the platform and plunged into the river. It was completed in 1891 and, just as the engineers planned, the water flowed. But the gold didn't. The gold flecks were too fine to be sluiced profitably. The chief engineer of the project committed suicide, and the flume was left to rot on the walls of Mesa Canyon. Sections of the flume are still visible today, rotting slowly in the dry desert air, a monument to greed and to the hard way that dreams sometimes die.

At Muleshoe Bend the river swings a wide loop, almost coming back into itself downstream. The crew takes the high road, hiking up and over the thin mesa that separates the two channels. The four boatmen take the boats around the bend to meet them.

Alone, drifting with the boat around the bend, I think about this trip. We came to celebrate a river. But it is too early to say what will happen to the Dolores River when the gates of the McPhee Dam close. Other rivers have survived their dams—the Gunnison River in the Gorge, the Green River through Lodore, the Colorado River in the Grand Canyon. But this is different, more personal. We never knew those rivers before the dams; those are memories that belong to other times. We've run the Dolores and seen it in its prime spring-time form. We know Spring Canyon Rapid, Molar, Canine, Snaggle-tooth and the way the water curls against the walls of Slickrock Canyon at sunset. This loss will be our loss, something we will carry in our own eyes the rest of our lives.

Maybe they are right, those who say the river, with its clear water, trout fishing, river otters and longer rafting season, will be a better place to raft. Maybe, but it will not be the same. It will never be the same.

A tug of current twists my oar and I look up to see the other rafts already far downstream picking up the hikers. I do know that some-where there have to be rivers that flow free, if only to remind us of what has been lost. I pull hard on the oars to catch up. A canyon wren calls from somewhere in the cliffs, a song that flows like water and then slowly fades to silence.

9.

FLATHEAD RIVER

MIDDLE FORK

Robert C. Gildart

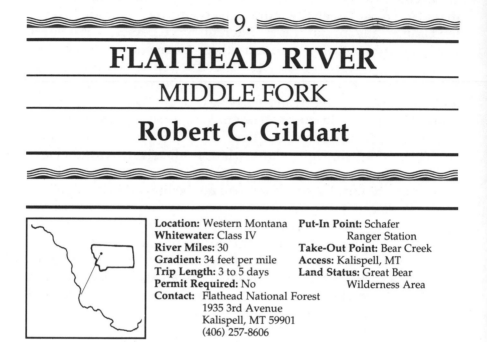

Location: Western Montana
Whitewater: Class IV
River Miles: 30
Gradient: 34 feet per mile
Trip Length: 3 to 5 days
Permit Required: No
Contact: Flathead National Forest
1935 3rd Avenue
Kalispell, MT 59901
(406) 257-8606

Put-In Point: Schafer
Ranger Station
Take-Out Point: Bear Creek
Access: Kalispell, MT
Land Status: Great Bear
Wilderness Area

Spruce Park, a section of Montana's 60-mile-long Middle Fork of the Flathead River, is a river rat's delight. It is a several-mile-long stretch of water laced with sinkholes, standing waves, whirlpools and hundreds of boulders that challenge equipment and a rafter's skills. No gradual easing into the frothing waters here. Suddenly oarsmen are gripped in the river's brawny hold. Water punches over bows, whirling crafts into eddies and thrusting them back into the major force of the current.

Invariably, when approaching Spruce Park in my 14-foot raft, I have been lured forward by sheer cliffs covered with ferns and dappled with variegated flowers—mindless of the robust waters. And always I have found myself careening wildly between waves, bouncing over rocks and slamming into slate-sided cliffs.

For a number of years I have been enamored by the Middle Fork, in part because of the challenge of the untamed and unpredictable sections. But I am also drawn to all aspects of a wilderness waterway. The upper portion of the Middle Fork offers such an immersion. Here the river passes through the Great Bear Wilderness, which in turn is nestled between Glacier National Park and the Bob Marshall Wilderness.

Through the 1970s, the Great Bear represented an emotionally charged battleground between those for and those against the idea of endowing the area with wilderness status. The proponents won and today the Great Bear remains pristine, protecting a river whose headwaters are as interesting to reach as the river is exciting to run. In fact, some say the Middle Fork is one of the most exhilarating of the Northwest's rivers.

History helps support this contention. Listen for a moment to the facts: The river has toppled horses and riders end-over-end. It has uprooted wilderness cabins, altered stream courses and once bowed a bridge entrance to Glacier National Park. But approached properly in a raft, the river can be navigated, leaving indelible memories and earning lasting praise. Said one Northwest concessionaire, "The Middle Fork may offer the most diverse river experience in the West." By that I have come to understand that the Middle Fork is wild, the fishing superb and the surroundings magnificent.

The headwaters of the Middle Fork can be reached—if toting a 100-pound raft and assorted gear—only by pack animal or light plane. Last summer our party chartered a Cessna to fly into a small, grass-covered airstrip. Before descending between snow-covered mountains, our pilot circled the strip to be sure it was clear of moose. Moments after landing we were loading our gear into Forest Service wheelbarrows, available from nearby Schafer Ranger Station.

Schafer is an old ranger station, thought to have been manned since the early 1950s. In 1987, the log buildings were occupied by Dick LaVanway, once a packer but now a forest technician who took time to point out a moose licking at a nearby salt block.

"Look there," LaVanway said. "That moose and her calf have sent more than one pilot back up over the Swan Range. Wildlife gets priority here, but partly because the critters demand it. Who wants to battle a moose?"

A portion of LaVanway's job was to register floaters, provide the poorly-prepared with maps, and offer advice and suggestions. He doesn't check out a floater's equipment. By the time rafters arrive at Schafer, it is much too late for evaluations. Planes are airborne moments after they touch the ground. Passengers remain to either walk out or raft out from the heart of the wilderness.

After a short haul from the ranger station, we gathered a few miles below the confluence of Bowl and Strawberry creeks, the origin of the Middle Fork. It was early, and dew covered the grass and stalks of thimbleberry, alder and willow that flanked the river. The sun was hidden by the mountains spiraling high to the east. The sky was a deep blue and the clear river reflected the color as the water passed quietly by. The river was a painfully cold. We grimaced as we stepped into the snowmelt and pushed our raft from the shore.

As the day progressed, the river picked up volume. Schafer, Morrison and Granite creeks added water as did Castle, Lunch and Long creeks. Still, the Middle Fork remained relatively calm. Other than the kaleidoscoping landscape, the only significant change was the size of the boulders. They were huge and we regretted that we could not have floated in mid-June, only a few weeks earlier, when the water was considerably higher.

Compounding the problem was the summer's dryness. But the fishing remained good, and several in our group of eight were avid anglers. The fish we caught were the aggressive westslope cutthroat trout, a species which the wilderness designation may have saved.

When the battle over the designation was being fought, Montana Senator Lee Metcalf said, "The westslope cutthroat has been reduced to threatened species status due to destruction of spawning habitat throughout its former range. . . .the survival of this native trout species and other important sport fish in the Flathead River system is dependent on the protection of the upper Middle Fork watershed."

To test the effectiveness of conservation methods on this species of trout, my son David and I waded waist-deep into the Middle Fork to fish. On one line was a gray wolf, on the other, a black gnat. Within moments we were fighting angry westslope cutthroats that pirouetted along the water's surface, leaped through the air, then re-entered the water. Rods bent; two-pound leaders strained. Some fish were netted while others escaped. That day we stopped early, anxious to continue fishing a particularly promising series of holes. Later, our party prepared for a fish dinner over a bed of coals. The river was living up to its image. So, we soon discovered, was the Great Bear Wilderness.

One attraction of floating the upper section of the Middle Fork was that the trip could be a leisurely one. From Schafer Meadow to the take-out at Bear Creek is only about 30 miles. On a five-day jaunt like ours, that left time for hiking a few of the many trails that weave throughout the area.

Early one morning we departed for Moose Lake, where we encountered fresh grizzly tracks. Apparently the bear had wandered this trail several hours earlier, seeking to quench its thirst or stalk the river's shores for fish. The Great Bear Wilderness was established primarily to provide free-ranging grizzly bears with the habitat they needed to roam unhindered between the Bob Marshall Wilderness and Glacier National Park. This 285,700-acre chunk of land provided the missing link.

But the Great Bear also preserves a variety of other species. During our trip we saw deer, elk, waterfowl and other birds normally found in pristine waterways. One intriguing bird was the water ouzel or dipper. This species protects its young by constructing nests in only the wildest of areas: behind waterfalls or along the banks of raging rivers.

On the Middle Fork we saw a number of water ouzels perched atop rocks, searching the frothy water at their feet for food. When a morsel was sighted the ouzels would enter the water and probe the bottom, then return to the surface, flit to a rock and devour the food.

For long stretches on the Middle Fork, we simply drifted in the rafts, talking among ourselves, applying sunscreen, watching the wildlife and anticipating the whitewater ahead. We had glimpsed only hints of the river's reputation. Just above Morrison Creek, the Three Forks Series had bounced my 15-year-old son from his perch on the raft's stern. Again, we wondered about the river's potential energy. Soon we encountered some answers.

About mid-afternoon we passed a steep-faced cliff that jutted upward about 30 feet, then angled and formed a platform. On the platform was perched a log cabin. Lou Bruno, a member of our party, told us that the cabin was uprooted and washed downstream by the flood of 1964, one of the valley's unparalleled natural disasters.

"Imagine," said Bruno, "waters so savage they can rip a cabin from its moorings, send it careening several miles downstream and then plant it on a cliff 20 feet higher than we are now floating. . . .My

God, I wouldn't have wanted to be here then."

Statistically, the flood that uprooted the cabin was one that should occur only once every 100 years. Satisfied with these predictions and the cabin's new location, the Forest Service has since provided the building with a new foundation and has constructed a series of corrals.

From the shade provided by the eaves of the old cabin we heard the water's roar in the canyon below. Downstream toward Spruce Park, spray glistened in the afternoon sun, creating a panoply of colors that combined to form multi-layered rainbows.

The next and last day we arose early. The map indicated that we were approaching Spruce Park. Much of the river's wildness is the result of its steep gradient. It drops an average of 34 feet per mile from its headwaters to Bear Creek. Through the Spruce Park area, a four-mile section of the stream drops an average of 41 feet per mile. This is the section anticipated by whitewater enthusiasts, and it is the one that has caused me problems. Depending on the volume of runoff, this area sometimes produces waters in the Class V category and is considered extremely difficult to navigate. We were barely in the water before a relentless roar assaulted our ears, warning us of wild water and dredging up memories.

Once, I recalled, the waves had hurtled my large raft like a frisbee, spinning us from one of the passage's high narrow walls to the other. Another time the waters had planted the bow of the craft on water-rounded rocks, where passengers remained helpless as waves poured over the raft's low trailing edge. Only by rocking the raft could we inch our way back into the main flow, where once again the oarsman plied his skills against a river that is never the same.

This time we paddled cautiously, peering ahead in search of the source of the roar. We found it at a tortuous bend in a narrow canyon where the water gushed into the side of a wall and then folded back over on itself. A relatively short stretch downstream we could see relief from the turbulence in the form of a sandy beach. We paddled vigorously for the opening, planning to pull over and line the rafts down from the beach.

At the last minute we decided to plunge on. Orienting the rafts so that the bows pointed upstream, we paddled against the current, pulling with all of our strength, trying to counter the surging water and avoid having it carry us with it and slam us into the cliff face.

Raft one maneuvered past the area artfully; raft two was not as successful, grazing the side and shipping a bit of water. Still, all in all, it was a successful passage—our first through Spruce Park.

From Spruce Park to the take-out at Bear Creek near Highway 2 is about eight miles. At the confluence the river continues, forming the eastern boundary of Glacier National Park. For 40 miles or more the Middle Fork flows freely, passing by incredibly spectacular country. But this section is not a wilderness river. That designation is proper only for the upper portion, where two sections combine to form a great unified corridor. That portion is a wild place where man's thoughts revolve around fish, bears and unpredictable waters, where man is but an occasional visitor, where the Great Bear Wilderness surrounds and isolates an unparalleled section of the Middle Fork of the Flathead River.

10

THE GREEN RIVER

LODORE CANYON

Jeff Rennicke

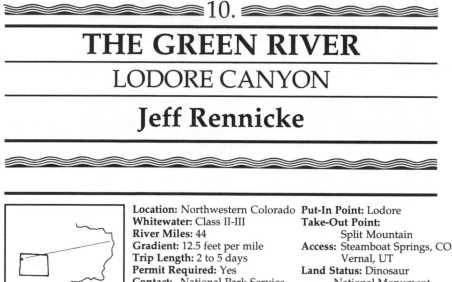

Location: Northwestern Colorado
Whitewater: Class II-III
River Miles: 44
Gradient: 12.5 feet per mile
Trip Length: 2 to 5 days
Permit Required: Yes
Contact: National Park Service,
Dinosaur National Monument
P.O. Box 210, Dinosaur, CO 81618
(303) 374-2216

Put-In Point: Lodore
Take-Out Point:
Split Mountain
Access: Steamboat Springs, CO
Vernal, UT
Land Status: Dinosaur
National Monument

It had been a long, tough week. Camped at the confluence of the Green and Yampa rivers, Major John Wesley Powell looked back on the dark canyon he and his men had just been spewed out of. Writing in his trip log for June 17, 1869, he called the whole ordeal "a chapter of disaster and toil." He had his reasons.

In the seven days in Lodore Canyon, the men of the most historic river trip in history had managed to put only about 20 river miles behind them. One boat, the *No Name*, was lost, or more poetically as Powell put it, first "broken quite in two" and then "dashed to pieces" on the rocks of what would be forever after known as Disaster Falls. Another boat, the *Maid of the Canyon*, was almost lost when a rope snapped. Long strings of rapids required portaging over the slippery rocks. Much of the mess kit and nearly the cook were lost in a panic when sparks from the cooking fire set the camp ablaze.

By the time Powell sat writing in his journal from the camp at Echo Park, the trip was just 24 days into what would be 100 days on the river. Of the three men involved in the wreck of the *No Name,* one man, Frank Goodman, resolved to leave the trip at the earliest opportunity and the other two, the Howland brothers, were so shaken that they would later desert the trip at the head of another major falls in the famous Separation Rapid incident. From the sketchy information Powell had been able to gather about the journey, he knew, even at Echo Park, that the worst whitewater was still downstream. For three days Powell and his men camped there along the Green River, fixing broken gear, taking scientific readings and gathering their courage like so much wind-scattered seed.

The beauty of this canyon is powerful stuff. Despite all the trouble, Powell and his men were struck by the scenery, describing it as "beyond the power of the pen to tell." In fact, they were so moved that even this wind-hardened bunch turned to poetry in naming the canyon. They called it Lodore after an 19th-century poem by Robert Southey.

Though the Flaming Gorge Dam upstream has throttled the rapids a bit, Powell and his men would still be struck by the wild beauty that has remained in Lodore Canyon nearly 120 years later.

Most river put-ins are merely convenient, a place where the roads happen to nudge up against the river for a bit. But if Lodore Canyon is poetry, then the first couplet is not far from the put-in. If you can ignore the usual bureaucratic signposts and the prefabricated living quarters of the rangers, the view is spectacular as soon as you push off into the current. It is this view that shook Powell, who called it "a dark portal to a region of doom." Before him the Ashley Expedition had seen it and anticipated "a dreadful termination of our voyage." There, just downstream from the launch site, the cliffs rise on either side of the river like hands folding for prayer: the Gates of Lodore.

Today, passing through the gates is a kind of initiation into the river world. It is a passage not into a region of doom but into the world of the Green River. A hundred years can do somersaults with perspective.

The rafts ahead are crossing to the other side of the river where a sliver of morning sun has hit the water. It is early in the season, April, and there are still pockets of snow on some of the shaded spots along the river, but the sun is warm and we begin to thaw out. The two kayakers thrash like maniacs back and forth trying to get the blood flowing.

The Green River begins more than 200 miles to the north, flowing off the Wind River Mountains of Wyoming. On its course through the landscape and through time it has carried many names. The Crow Indians called it *Seedskeedee*, the Prairie Hen River. It has been called the Snake and the South Bitterroot at times; now it is just called the Green.

Just as we start to warm up, we pull to the right shore and hike up a slit in the canyon called Winnies Grotto, named for the daughter of the geologist on Powell's second expedition. It looks like nothing so much as the scar from a giant axe, only a few feet wide at the bottom, wedge-shaped and filled with air so cold that the sun must never reach here. "Hell of a thing to name after your daughter," I think, hiking into the dark shadows.

At the farthest reaches, up where the meltwater has been dripping in from above, there is a natural ice sculpture, surprisingly graceful and delicate, but the sight of it sends the cold rushing back into my bones. Still, I stand looking at it long after the others have headed back for the sunshine. I recall a sketch of the grotto reproduced in the *Powell Journals*, a book I carry in my river library, and head down to compare it with the canyon as it looks today. I hold the book up as we float on downriver. The lines are not exact, the artist's hand may have taken poetic liberties with the steepness, but there is no doubting that this is the place. I look out over more than 100 years, but for all the difference in the grotto it could be a single day.

Despite the fact that the 502-foot cement plug upstream known as the Flaming Gorge Dam backed the river up for 91 miles when it closed its gates in 1964, the men of the Powell party would still recognize the river's unmistakable pull to the sea. Just after the stop at Winnies Grotto, the pull becomes a tug. For the next 10 miles the river drops 222 feet, creating the biggest whitewater in the canyon.

Some 35 feet of the drop are made at the point of Powell's dilemma, Disaster Falls. As we scout along the left bank, I am still carrying the *Powell Journals* and I notice that there is also a sketch of Disaster Falls. I hold it up to the rapid but my eyes can't make the 100-year jump like they did at the grotto. The dam has tamed the water and the sketch seems of another place. Tom Beck, another of the boatmen, and I stroll along the length of the rapid before turning back to the boats. "Not much," he says and then, as if recalling something or suddenly imagining what it once must have been, adds "now."

We walk back in silence and run the rapid, all three of the rafts and both kayaks coming through cleanly. No one says it out loud, but there is the feeling of something lost even before we had a chance to know it.

We flow through the heart of Dinosaur National Monument, and on the flatwater I daydream about the dinosaurs. The climate must have been much different then, but even in the recent past this high desert has seen enough cattle, sheep, cattle rustlers and sheep rustlers to raise a cloud of dust clear to the Wyoming line. It is said that Lodore Canyon has seen the bootprints of the likes of Butch Cassidy and the Sundance Kid, Flatnose Curry and the hermit of the canyons, Pat Lynch.

Still, none of them could claim more grit than one Queen Ann Bassett. The "queen" was a hard-living, hard-riding woman whose fatal flaw was that she tended to make her living with other folks' stock. One night, it is said, Queen Ann, pursued by a posse, drove a whole herd of borrowed cattle off a cliff at Zenobia Creek. To this day, the ripples of this stretch of river are said to be the struggles of Queen Ann's cattle making for shore.

Just downstream we pull off to make camp. Steak for dinner, and all night I hear in my dreams the sounds of cattle splashing in the river. The morning rises slowly, as if chipping its way through the frost that covers our sleeping bags and hangs like white whiskers on the boats. Jerry Mallett, "Ol Hardbark," is up making coffee and, even in this cold, wearing only a pair of shorts and a T-shirt from Ray's Tavern that says Have A Nice Day A——— on one side and Patience Hell, I Want To Kill Somebody on the other.

The *Powell Journals* and the way the years have treated this canyon are still on my mind. Jerry has been running rivers for nearly two decades and ran Lodore 16 years ago, so I ask him if it looks any different. He looks up from the coffee, now steaming on the fire, considers a moment, and then says, "Yeah, the walls look a little higher." I guess I should know better than to expect insight this early in the morning.

It is cold but the sun rises over the canyon and warms the day before we shove off.

It is times like this that I hate guidebooks and maps. In places, Lodore still seems as wild as the day Powell laid eyes on it; even the

jet contrails look like thin clouds if you squint hard enough. The day
has the feel of newness and that we are the first ones to set foot here.
Still, there is the thought of the dam, the line across the river on the
maps. No matter how exciting Triplet Falls or Hells-Half-Mile turn
out to be, there will remain the questions: What was it like for
Powell? What did it seem like to Ashley? It is like a cloud over the
day.

Triplet does little to dispel the cloud. But Hells-Half-Mile, churning in the early spring runoff, seems big to me. It is wilder than I
thought it would be. On a big rock a ways out into the river, Beck and
I sit and discuss the rapid with all the seriousness of a first run. It
seems unruly enough to earn its title and for a moment the dam is
forgotten, the guidebooks don't matter and the years melt like ice.

A huge hole is planted in its gut like a bully in a doorway. There
is a good half-mile of rapid below the rock, but it is the boulder that
sucks our attention the way it sucks the water into it. There is no talk
of what this rapid once was or even a hint of parody in our scouting.
The twang in our gut as we check the rigging and go through our
own little pre-rapid rituals is as real as rock and as hard.

The kayakers decide to strap their boats onto the rafts and ride
this one out. "Too cold," they say in unison like a planned alibi, but
there is no need for excuses at this place. We strap them on and run,
all the boats getting through safely, but with a new respect for the
Green River and its power and beauty. There may be more here than
the guidebooks can tell.

At Echo Park we float around the mountain of slickrock called
Steamboat Rock and see the Yampa River flowing in from the east.
Powell and his men named this place Echo Park for the "magical
music" of the echoes given off by the cliffs; I think of the journal of
one of the boatmen on Powell's second expedition, which tells of
rowing up the Yampa River from here at midnight under a full
moon, singing. We don't sing; instead, we scan the cliffs and listen.
In a special project of the National Park Service and the Colorado Di-
vision of Wildlife, peregrine falcons have been reintroduced to the
Monument and nest on the cliffs above Echo Park. I'd rather see a
peregrine on the wing than listen to the sound of my own voice.

Below the confluence, the Green River, flowing heavy now from
the added weight of the Yampa, winds its way into Whirlpool
Canyon. It is named as much for the swirling rock types as for the
current. Much of Whirlpool Canyon is quietwater, but in the walls

is a rapid of rock formations, the most diverse along the river—
Morgan sandstone, Mississippian and Pennsylvanian strata, the
Lodore formation, Lodgepole and Deseret limestones, even some-
thing known as the Humbug formation.

At Jones Hole, the side creek is raging so full of fury from the
warm weather that we have to cross it balanced on a log like wire-
walkers to hike up the canyon to the pictographs. Of all the rock art
in the Southwest the pictographs of Jones Hole are among the best—
stick-like figures, bighorn sheep, snakes. But the ones that haunt my
mind are the simplest: handprints where a Fremont Indian laid his
palm against the cold rock of the cliff 1,500 years ago,

Jones Hole is our last camp. We row the 19 miles of river through
Greasy Pliers Rapid and the still waters of Island Park, searching the
walls for a petroglyph of a buffalo that is somewhere on these cliffs.
Then, as if in a last stand, the river drops through a quick succession
of rapids called SOB, Moonshine, Schoolboy and Inglesby. Just three
miles later, we are at the Split Mountain take-out.

The Green River through Dinosaur National Monument has
changed in the hundred years since Powell and his men explored its
beauty and fought with its rapids. And it has stayed the same. What
would the men of that expedition recognize—the grotto? Echo Park?
Would they still feel the power of Hells-Half-Mile and Disaster
Falls? The questions make good conversation around a pitcher of
beer at Ray's Tavern in Green River, a hangout for boatmen. When
someone pushes G-57 on the jukebox and plays John Prine's "Paradise," I think of Lodore. It is a different Green River that the song
speaks of when it says:

"Down by the Green River where Paradise lay. . . . " But Paradise
is a subjective thing and besides, there is not a boatman in the place
whose mind is not drifting back to Whirlpool Canyon or SOB Rapid.
It's close enough to Paradise for me and so I can't help but sing along,
out of tune and loud.

11

THE GREEN RIVER

DESOLATION CANYON

Jeff Rennicke

Location: Central Utah
Whitewater: Class II-Class III
River Miles: 84
Gradient: 7 feet per mile
Trip Length: 4 to 5 days
Permit Required: Yes
Contact: Bureau of Land Management
River Unit
P.O. Drawer AB, Price, UT
(801) 634-4584

Put-In Point: Sand Wash
Take-Out Point: Swasey's Rapid
Access: Green River, UT
Ouray, UT
Land Status: BLM, Uintah
Indian Reservation

If I could dream a river trip, it would begin with a sunset. One where the whole western horizon is ablaze with reds and oranges and a yellow like the clear flames of burning driftwood. It would be one of those skies that changes just slightly every time you look away and, when you close your eyes, can never quite be remembered fully. It would linger long into the twilight, glowing quietly like the last embers of the night's campfire, the stars appearing above it like sparks. If I could dream a river trip, it would begin with a sunset like the one tonight as we drive the dusty canyons of the Green River to a place the maps call Desolation.

The sunset has been snubbed out and it is dark when we reach the end of the long dirt road that leads to the river and a place called Sand Wash. The slice of moon in the sky is so thin it looks like a long, skinny star against the shadows of the cottonwoods; its light is as effective as a single firefly. "Man, it's black," someone says, unloading the rafts and groping around on the floor of the van as if trying to read a huge sheet of Braille. "That's good," I answer, "maybe the mosquitoes won't be able to find us in the dark." Wrong.

The mosquitoes of Sand Wash are legendary, rivaling the tall tales of their Alaskan cousins or those of Minnesota, where the mosquito is considered the state bird. They are major league, big-time bugs these mosquitoes, the kind that can carry off small dogs and use a wooden oar for a toothpick. Their buzzing has all the tune of a chain saw and at night, even though the skies are clear, the sound of them plinking against the tent has me dreaming of rain.

By morning the swarms of bugs have shrunk from legendary down to only amazing, most of them chased off by the heat, but there are still enough to quicken the pace of rigging the boats. We are pumped up, packed and paddling before the sun is very far over the lip of the canyon. As soon as we are on the water the memory of the bugs trails off like a shout up a box canyon, and for the rest of the trip I don't see another of the Sand Wash savages.

The Green River through Desolation Canyon begins slowly, very slowly. For the first 26 miles the waters of the river are as smooth and unruffled as the slickrock walls of the canyon. It is a time to settle in, to get the feel of the oars in your hand, to practice your roll in the kayak.

Because of this first quiet stretch of water and the way the rapids downstream start easy and build into successively more challenging water, Desolation Canyon is a perfect place for beginning kayakers and rafters to break into river running. The kayakers in our party splash around the rafts like colorful dolphins playing in the wake of a ship, spraying us with water. When they tire of the game and paddle off, their voices fade into silence. A raven flies low over the river, the air across its wings rattling like wind through a bunch of dry sticks.

Jasmine looks up curiously at the raven as it passes, twisting around so much to watch it that she almost tumbles off the tube and into the bottom of the boat. Since we have so many kayakers, I am running the baggage boat. Jasmine is my only passenger, a big, yellow and overly friendly dog. Each time I bring my camera up to my eye, she insists on sniffing the lens so that by the end of the trip I have more pictures than I could ever want of the black, wet end of Jasmine's snout.

Drifting through the canyon is like drifting through a book of canyon geology. Not far from the put-in is Gothic Cathedral. Farther on is Sumner's Amphitheater. All along the river's course there are formations like Lighthouse Rock, arches and strange, statue-like rocks called hoodoos that stand like the sentinels to some forgotten castle. It is a playground for the winds and time.

The most interesting formations to me are not the most startling; they would never make a great postcard. They are the empty canyons called rincons, like the one at Tabyago Canyon. Rincons mark the places where the river once swooped in great bends, until they were abandoned as the river cut a straighter course. Where the river once flowed sits an empty shell with the eeriness of a ruin, a great bone hollowed out and bleaching in the sun. Now there is are only an empty canyon and the wind echoing now and again with a sound hauntingly like that from an old shell held quietly to the ear.

To the eyes of Major John Wesley Powell and his men on their famous 1869 journey, the strange shadows and odd formations made it "a region of the wildest desolation" and so this subtle, beautiful place became known as Desolation Canyon.

Shadows slip across the river as we paddle far into the late afternoon, putting miles behind us. The day passes dream-like with the unbroken flow of the flatwater and the canyon walls shimmering in the heat. We make camp on a sandy beach at river left. I climb on the ledges above camp to photograph the river in the last light. The rock has been shattered into flat tiles that clatter with every step, and the sound startles a pair of scraggly mule deer as I top the last ledge. The river beyond stretches out in great bends—flat green and endless. Far off, on the river flats below, I catch a last glimpse of the mule deer. Like the river, they are still moving.

By mid-morning the skyline is dominated by Lighthouse Rock, which also signals the beginning of the whitewater in Desolation. At Jack Creek, the river comes to life. The rapids become more frequent, each one growing into a low growl that shatters the silence from upstream—Jack Creek, Firewater, Cedar Ridge and other riffles without names. The first large rapid is Steer Ridge. We stop and scout— a large entry wave, rocky channels below teeming with small holes and a larger hole at the bottom.

Just below Steer Ridge lies a small, nameless place where Powell and his men capsized, one of several mishaps they had in this canyon that might have colored their view in naming the place Desolation.

Rock Creek, flowing clear as mountain air off the West Tavaputs Plateau and home to a small population of rainbow trout, seems anything but desolate as we cool off in the shaded waters. Downstream, where our camp sits on a sandy beach scattered with cottonwoods and our dinner of chicken and rice simmers in the dutch oven, desolation is not a word that comes readily to mind. Some outfitters have gone to calling Desolation the Green River Wilderness to keep passengers from shying away at its name. The canyon itself takes no notice of whatever it says on the maps, and the sun reflecting tonight off the rock walls has the river running the same shade of gold.

There is another kind of writing in the canyon, not on the maps, but in the rock. Scattered up and down the canyon like ancient echoes are pictographs, made by drawing on the rock surface with other colored rocks or with dyes made from roots, and petroglyphs, which are pecked into the cliffs with harder rocks. Distinct shapes like desert bighorn, human figures and snakes dance among abstract drawings like patterns of dreams or visions. Whole walls are riddled with the drawings.

The art is the work of the Fremont Indians who lived in these canyons until about 800 years ago. Their language cannot be read by modern eyes. Some think the figures represent religious offerings; some think they are the product of idle hands passing a rainy day. Whatever they are, pictographs and petroglyphs are as close as we will ever come to hearing these ancient voices. Whenever we come across them there is a moment of silence in the group, as if each of us is straining to hear the distant echo.

There is no trouble hearing the river boiling through its rapids on this lower stretch of Desolation Canyon—Moonwater Rapid, Red Point, Joe Hutch. Where the water quiets for a time, on a large, grassy flat on river left sits the McPherson Ranch. If the old beams and cactus could talk they would tell stories of the days when Butch Cassidy and his Wild Bunch used the ranch as a hide-out and resting place. It is not far downstream, near Rattlesnake Rapids, that Flat Nose Curry of the Wild Bunch found his final resting place, killed by a posse during the winter of 1899 to 1900.

Recently, the Ute Indians have taken over the lodge with plans for a campground and store, but today it is as silent as it must have been the day after the Wild Bunch rode off for the last time.

Just below McPherson Ranch, Desolation Canyon itself fades to silence as we make camp out on the wide flat below Florence Creek.

Strangely enough the most difficult of the rapids so far on the river lie here, outside the deep heart of the canyon: Three Fords.

Named for the three channels of the river once forded by cattle during long drives, Three Fords turns the river into a maze. Under a hot sun that lights the canyon like a flame, we scout and then run the left and deepest channel. The swells lift the boat high and then drop it hard as if on the back of some unbroken mud-colored horse.

On the flatwater below, our boats drift slowly between the rising walls of another canyon, Gray Canyon. As with so many places along the rivers in the Southwest, Gray Canyon owes its name to the men of the Powell Expedition and, more specifically, to a dust storm that kicked up huge, billowing clouds of gray dust while the expedition was camped here.

For us, the sky is clear and the wind still as we run the big holes of Coal Creek, considered the river's premier rapid. At Coal Creek, the walls on the right bank near the head of the rapid wear a long, vertical scar—the remnant of a dam project gone bust before it could still the waters of the canyon. Not far below, almost hidden in the shadows, a mule deer doe and fawn stare out from the trees and turn their heads slowly as our boats drift downstream and out of sight.

We make our final camp on the river upstream from Nefertiti Rapid near a small, nameless riffle that we swim through in our life jackets again and again, riding the swells like windblown leaves in a brown sky.

Late, when it is nearly too dark to see or do anything about it, a storm kicks up. It is a dry storm with no rain but with winds that seem as hot and puckered as an old man's breath. Some of the boatmen run around trying to put up tents and tarps as the storm rattles in the branches of the cottonwoods overhead. But there is no rain, just the canyon winds getting tangled in the dark. Before the last of the tents are up and secured, the winds have untangled and subsided to a whisper without a single drop of rain. The winds return to wherever they came from, and the rest of the night is still and quiet. The stars overhead seem sharp enough to etch the sky like scratched glass.

By morning the only signs of the storm are a few clouds and a layer of dust that dulls everything left out last night—the rafts, the kayaks, the kitchen gear. Everything looks bland, colorless gray, even the canyon walls. The first splash of Nefertiti Rapid puts the life back in the boats; the first wind puts the color back in the cliffs.

Just downstream of Nefertiti, a jeep road joins the river and follows it the rest of the way to our take-out at Swaysey's Rapid. By the time we gather the gear, deflate the boats and load the truck, all the time hopping like lizards across the hot sands at Swaysey's beach, the sun is nearly down.

If I could dream a river trip, it would end with a sunset where the sky glows as if all the stars had gone red and slipped to the western edge of the sky, a sunset that hangs in the sky almost until morning. But it doesn't happen. Even though there are a few clouds left over from last night's hard blow, the sun drops from the horizon like an egg slipping off a hot skillet. It is just gone, like we are down the long road home. Dreams can't be expected to come true every time, at least not in a place with a name like Desolation.

12

GREEN RIVER/ COLORADO RIVER

LABYRINTH CANYON/ CATARACT CANYON

Jeff Rennicke

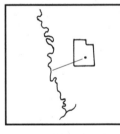

Location: Central Utah
Whitewater: Class I-IV
River Miles: 163
Gradient: 1 to 25 feet per mile
Trip Length: 5 days
Permit Required: Yes
Contact: Canyonlands National Park
Moab, UT 84532
(801) 259-7165.

Put-In Point: Green River
State Park
Take-Out Point: Hite Marina
Access: Green River, UT
Land Status: BLM,
Canyonlands National Park

When the jukebox in Ray's Tavern goes quiet between songs, you can almost hear the roar of it. The walls are crammed with pictures of it—triple-rigs waffling in the towering waves of Big Drop, kayaks looking like toothpicks against the teeth of Satan's Gut, a dory burrowing into the brown fists of the waves at Mile Long. Talk around the bar overflows with stories about it. A drawing of it graces the T-shirt of a player at the free pool table. It is the place that defines bigwater boating in the West. At high flows it has the biggest waves found anywhere on the Colorado River. This is the place. "Cat," the boatmen call it, Cataract Canyon.

74

Out behind Ray's Tavern, in the shade of the huge cottonwood trees that mark the boat launch at Green River State Park, the river is quiet. It flows cat-like around the legs of Randy Fabres as he wades out to check the ropes and make final adjustments on the boat he and I will share on this trip, a small, 12-foot Fiberglas dory called an Ouzel that he made himself in his New Mexico workshop. It is so new that Randy still has fiberglass splinters under his fingernails. It is a beautiful, delicate boat the color of the canyon walls and it floats in the slight current as easily as light upon the water. Still, as we push off into the current, I can't help thinking about how small it looks beside the rafts and about those pictures on the tavern wall.

Riding a dory for the first time is like riding a bubble. It has a motion closer to a canoe or a kayak than to a raft, and it seems to dance on the water. Randy is an experienced doryman. I'll have just the 100 miles of flatwater to get to know the dance before the whitewater of Cataract. We are coming at Cat from a little different angle. Most trips start at Moab on the Colorado River. We start on the Green and float the 117 miles of Labyrinth and Stillwater Canyons before we meet the Colorado River at the gateway to Cat, the Confluence.

In the years since I came to the West I have thought about getting to the Confluence. I've traced the lines of the Colorado and the Green on maps until they blend together there in the middle of nowhere. I've seen old, dusty photographs. I've seen satellite shots that show the two great rivers of the Rocky Mountain West coming together like arcs of lightning. But I want to see it for myself, to stand at the very point where these two rivers come together and then flow on.

The dory is easier to pack and faster on the water than the rafts, so Randy and I are far ahead of the rest before we ship the oars to drift. For the first 18 miles the talk is of what lies far downstream—the Confluence, Canyonlands National Park, Cataract. But as we drift slowly around a wide left-hand bend we spot something that changes the subject. There, jutting out of a landscape that has been mostly broken rolling hills, rises Dellenbaugh's Butte, or The Anvil, or The Inkwell, depending on what map you're reading. It is an odd, layered butte with lines so perfect it seems sculpted. The Powell Expedition named Dellenbaugh's Butte for the 17-year-old artist accompanying their trip. I think of the young artist's eye wandering over the maze of lines in the walls, dreaming of lines so graceful and so perfect in his own work.

We drift by silently and see, just downstream, the beginning of Labyrinth Canyon, a place whose beauty makes us forget about anything downstream, almost. At Trin-Alcove the others have caught up and we all drift in silence. A canyon wren calls, the song skipping down the cliffs, its echo getting tangled in the mouths of the three sidecanyons that meet the river at Trin-Alcove. The Powell Expedition camped near here, naming Labyrinth Canyon and Trin-Alcove.

The lines of Labyrinth Canyon are pure artwork; I think about this as I scramble up the cliffs at Bowknot Bend, where the river swings a wide loop, almost coming back into itself. It is seven miles around by boat and less than a mile on foot, so some of us have crawled up across the saddle to meet the boats on the other side. I sit for a long time at the high point letting my eyes float over the landscape like a raven on wind.

Labyrinth and Stillwater below are sandstone canyons that have been carved, chiseled and chipped by wind and rain for thousands of years into a strange collection of geologic formations—Dellenbaugh's Butte, Trin-Alcove, Bowknot Bend, The Butte of the Cross, The Sphinx, Turk's Head. Each of them seems somehow to give this empty land of restless browns and tans a form that is easier to grasp. On maps you go from one to the other like stepping stones, anchors in the landscape.

The others have hiked on ahead and the wind begins to moan in the cliffs, a deep and lonely sound like the wail of a coyote. Of all the landscapes that rivers flow through, the desert has always seemed to me the least human and somehow the most beautiful. Perhaps it is because of the surprise of finding a river of such great size here in all this space and light. Walk only a hundred yards up a sidecanyon and the thought of a river vanishes like an echo.

Maybe that's why there are so many pictographs and inscriptions carved in these canyon walls. They are a way of grasping, if only for a moment, a part of this place. Like old echoes carved in stone, the hands of those who came here before have left their mark trying to hold thet magic that a river has over the desert: D. Julien 1836, carved below Hey Joe Canyon and again at Hell Roaring Canyon, the Launch Marguerite inscription of 1909 on Spring Canyon Point, the old river register in the cliffs upstream, the cliff paintings and petroglyphs that dot the walls up many of the sidecanyons.

In the heart of Cataract Canyon there are the inscriptions of four expeditions from 1891 to 1940. There is even one from the ill-fated

Best Party that reads: Camp #7, Hell to Pay, No. 1 Sunk & Down. The silence here is deeper than the river; etchings in the stone give it an echo.

The thought of all of those inscriptions is comforting against the moaning of the wind and for a moment I consider carving my own name in the rocks at the saddle. But from around the bend upstream I see our boats coming now, all tied together and looking as tiny as a cottonwood leaf floating on the water. Someone has tied red and blue and yellow balloons to a pair of oars shipped as they drift toward camp. It seems a silly and beautiful gesture way out here, like carving your name in the wind. Even from this far off I can see the balloons dancing in the breeze, so I forget about the inscription and hike down to meet the boats at camp.

The pace of the river gets into your blood. Labyrinth Canyon is classic flatwater. The reeds along the riverbank hardly seem to bend with the current and it sets the tone for our trip. We drift slowly downstream, watching the clouds pass overhead. We stop for a time at the Outlaw Cabin once used as a hide-out by Butch Cassidy and the Wild Bunch. Some of us make the climb to the rim at Fort Bottom to stand and wonder at the slabrock tower built by the Anasazi, "the Ancient Ones." I sit for a time with my back against the tower, counting. Today, in this light, there are seven shades of blue in the desert sky. For days, through Labyrinth Canyon and Stillwater below, we drift as easily, slowly, as the play of light in this sky.

It is early morning when we near the Confluence. Randy and I pull out of camp before the shadows are even off the river and row hard for the first few miles. As it gets closer, we slow down and then stop rowing altogether to stretch out the last few riverbends. Great things always seem to happen too fast, and even though we are not rowing we suddenly round the last, long left-hand bend of the Green River. And then, there it is.

Both rivers carry about the same flow, doubling when the two become a single river. The joining occurs at a calm stretch of the river. Still, with the power inherent in the two rivers, there is a tangle of currents that whip like stormwinds where they meet. The dory shivers once as it hits the current, spins away and then settles to move off downstream. We are on the Colorado River.

The change is instantly apparent. The speed of the river picks up as if sliding off a cliff. Below, in Big Drops, the gradient picks up to over 30 feet in a single mile. Here it is less obvious, but then there is the sign: DANGER Cataract Canyon Hazardous Rapids 2 1/2 Miles. It doesn't get any more obvious than that.

We stop short of the main rapids, camp just below Spanish Bottom for a layover day, time to think about the rapids below and to explore Canyonlands National Park. It is a short climb from the river to a collection of spires and towers called The Doll House. Powell, in his journals, calls this section of the river a "land of naked rock." I walk alone among the formations, looking at them from all angles, trying to work them into various shapes in my mind. Maybe it is the thought of running the rapids tomorrow, but the towers of rock keep taking the shapes of waves in my mind and it is like a day spent walking a river gone to stone.

By mid-morning the next day, the waves are real and we are into the gut of Cataract. The river is high, running 44,000 cubic feet per second and carrying with it a deep-throated roar like thunder. There are 25 rapids in 12 miles of river, and at this level the rapids crowd into each other, forming stretches of almost continuous whitewater.

In the long runs of the first few rapids the dory comes alive. This is a craft built for whitewater and it dances through the rapids as if set to music, the blue sky overhead, the brown water below. The rapids here carry few names, they go by almost too quickly for that. They are simply given numbers—#6 and #7 flowing together with no break between, #9 coming at Tilted Park where the lines of the canyon go suddenly wild, #11 scraping around a small island that the river seems ready to wash away.

The stretch between #13 and #18 is called Mile Long and is one of the most exciting miles in river running. The run seems endless, one wave after the other, each one bigger than the last. As I crouch on the front of the dory, using my weight to highside against each wave, I can hear Randy laughing behind me as he rows. This is the big stuff.

Big Drop is even bigger. Big Drop is really made up of three rapids—#21, #22 and #23, also known as Big Drop One, Satan's Seat and Satan's Gut. From upstream it looks calm, as if the world just suddenly drops off a cliff in one glassy wave. We pull off to scout it on the left.

It is a long scout with difficult walking on rocks that seem too sharp and too hot to really be along a river. Most rapids are deceiving from shore. The waves always seem smaller than when you are staring them straight in the eye from the boat. Not at Big Drop. Here, the waves even look huge from shore. There on river right in Satan's Seat is a rock as big as a dragon that creates a pour-over big enough to lift the whole right side of the river and slam it down. It would be one of the worst places I've ever seen to put a boat.

Luckily, there is a rather obvious route through Big Drop, a place where there are only huge waves to worry about. After we've charted the course in our heads, Randy yells to me that it is time to run. The dory somehow seems even smaller drifting there in the eddy above the first drop. I get in a kneeling position in the bow where I'll be able to use my weight like ballast. Both of us are wearing kayak helmets and full wetsuits. It is going to be a wet ride.

The first wave hits us with more power than I thought it would and throws me off balance. In the little dory my weight is enough to shift us, but Randy compensates well until I am back in position. In the front of the dory my eyes are only three feet or so above the waterline, and from that vantage point the waves seem to tower, blocking out the view downstream as I stare straight into a wall of brick-colored water.

Time seems to speed up with the water. We are through the first drop almost before I feel myself breathing. I wish it were slower. I wish there was time to look around. There is no more beautiful and mesmerizing sight in any landscape than the swirl of water in a powerful rapid. It is like looking through a kaleidoscope—the way the waves build and break, the way the river tangles at the eddies, the play of light in the spray. From shore it is one-dimensional. From the bow of a boat it is like being surrounded by an orchestra.

I see the pour-over in Satan's Seat go by, looking as if the river were suddenly coming to a boil. We ride the tailwaves that lead out of this rapid and into Satan's Gut. We are almost through.

Then a wave turns the whole world dark and we are swimming just downstream of the overturned dory. I never saw the wave, only the shadow. The cold water is pouring in my wetsuit as I pull my arms against the current to reach the boat. It is like trying to walk against a tornado, but I manage to grab a gunwale. With hardly a tug, the self-bailing dory rolls upright. I kick my legs once to get in, but a wave crashes over me and rips the dory from my hand. I try again in the trough of the next wave and I am in, pulling Randy in behind me. He jumps to the oars to row but by this time we are almost through and there is nothing to do really but straighten the boat and ride it out.

In an eddy downstream we sit laughing, a nervous laugh shot through with the adrenaline still racing in our veins. We have to shout still to be heard over the rapids.

"The dory popped right back up," I say, still breathing hard.

"Just like it was supposed to," Randy says, obviously proud of the way the boat handled under pressure. "First time anyone ever beat me back into the driver's seat though."

"First time anyone was even a little more scared than you maybe," I say, still shaking from the cold water, from the fear and from the enormity of the power we were afloat in just a moment ago.

"Wonder if anyone got that on camera," Randy says after awhile, and I think again of the pictures on the wall at Ray's Tavern. They are awesome but they don't even come close, not even close.

For a long time neither one of us talks. We drift around in the eddy, feeling the sun warming the chill off our backs, thinking our own thoughts. Slowly I stop shaking. One of our rafts appears out of the rapids and then another. From the middle of the river, the oarsman of the last raft spins his boat to face upstream and raises his hand in a salute to the river. We push out of the eddy and follow the others downstream toward the take-out.

© Tom Beck

Colorado River, Grand Canyon, Arizona

© Tom Beck

Selway River, Idaho

© Mark Lorenzo

Cal Salmon River, California

© Jeff Rennicke

Colorado River, Utah/Arizona

© Jerry Mallett

Gunnison River, Gunnison Gorge, Colorado

© Verne Huser

Salmon River, Idaho

© David Bolling

American River, South Fork, California

© Larry Rice

Colorado River, Cataract Canyon, Utah

© Jeff Rennicke

Green River, Desolation Canyon, Utah

© Shelly Spalding

Deschutes River, Oregon

© Verne Huser

Skykomish River, Washington

© Larry Rice

Big Bend River, Texas

© Verne Huser

Snake River, Idaho

© Jeff Rennicke

Dolores River, Colorado

© Jeff Rennicke

Colorado River, Horsethief Canyon, Colorado

© Jeff Rennicke

Kobuk River, Alaska

13.

THE GUNNISON RIVER

GUNNISON GORGE

Jeff Rennicke

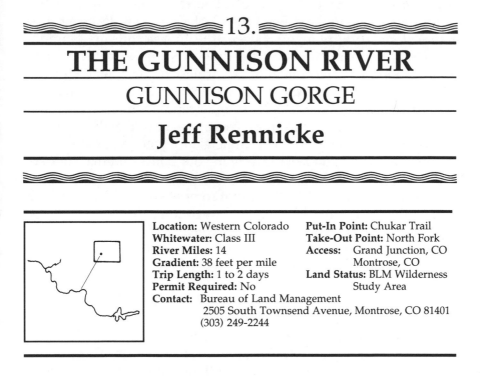

Location: Western Colorado
Whitewater: Class III
River Miles: 14
Gradient: 38 feet per mile
Trip Length: 1 to 2 days
Permit Required: No

Put-In Point: Chukar Trail
Take-Out Point: North Fork
Access: Grand Junction, CO
            Montrose, CO
Land Status: BLM Wilderness
            Study Area

Contact: Bureau of Land Management
            2505 South Townsend Avenue, Montrose, CO 81401
            (303) 249-2244

The dirt road ends, just stops like luck or a brick. As the truck rolls to a halt and the engine goes silent, we all sit for a moment in silence, looking around, not quite sure what comes next. There is a trail dropping off the plateau and winding out of sight between the piñons and the rock. There is wind and heat, but there is no river here. There are only a few hints where a river should be or even could be. Our pickup truck, filled with paddles and life jackets and wearing a canoe on its roof like a strange blue party hat, sits obediently as a lost horse patiently waiting in the shade for its rider who has been too long in the sun. I move first, trying to instill confidence, and start to unlash the canoe as if it is the most normal thing in the world to be doing on a dusty highland surrounded by sagebrush. Tom Beck, the leader of this trip, is not a man to get his bearings crossed. If he says there is a river here, then there is a river here. As I pull the canoe off the truck I think to myself, "I hope there is a river here."

One of the best ways to hide something of value is to roll it in a hole. If you want to hide a river there is no better hole than that crack in the earth of western Colorado called the Black Canyon of the Gunnison. A step to the edge of the Black Canyon is dizzying. The night-colored rocks plunge 2,800 feet, the highest cliffs in Colorado, and in places, like the Narrows, the canyon is only 40 feet wide. The combination of the steepness of the walls, the narrowness of the canyon and the angle of the rocks, which have been contorted and twisted, makes the canyon look like the aftermath of some unspeakable violence. Written into those rocks are more than 1.75 billion years of the earth's history. In a single glance your eyes scan a span of time that makes you feel the dust in your bones and that shatters your sense of scale like a rock.

Canoeing is not the first thing that comes to mind when you step to the edge of the Black Canyon; parachuting maybe. The Black Canyon is not a place for a canoe or even a raft for that matter. The Black Canyon is an expert-only run for people trained as much in rock climbing as in kayaking. In conversations between boatmen, the words *Black Canyon* mark the spot where all but the most hardcore kayakers among us tune out and go to the bar for another beer.

But there is another spot, the spot we've come to paddle, at a place just downstream of the famous Black Canyon where the walls bow down slightly and settle like waves after a storm. There is still the same Precambrian rock; there is still the same thin string of blue sky overhead. But there is a difference. The walls here are chipped more in grace than in strength and by the time the river flows out of the Black Canyon, a bit of the fight has gone out of it, just a bit. This is what we've come to paddle: the Gunnison Gorge.

With the first load we start down the trail, around boulders as big as heat-bloated horses, and through a narrow gap in the cliffs where the air smells like mountain lion and there are deer bones bleaching in the sun. The heat rises like dry smoke.

You can hear it before you see it. You can feel it before you hear it. Then, there it is, appearing like a gift around the last bend of the trail.

The Gunnison has come a long way to reach this point. Starting in the high country of Colorado's Sawatch Mountains, it flows through wild country most of its journey, picking up tributaries that come to it from the San Juan Mountains and the West Elks. It flows over a granite bed, picking up little sediment. Then it is strained through the dams of the Curecanti Project upstream, so that by the time the water reaches this point it is cold, clean, the color of river grass. We splash our faces with the water, sweet as sugar water, make another trip up the trail and then push our one canoe, one kayak and one paddleboat off into the current.

What strikes you first about the Gunnison is the water. There is an intrinsic beauty and fascination in the flow of pure water, the easy slide of river over moss-slickened rocks. Its movement is the movement of flames in a campfire, hypnotizing. It is never the same, curling cat-like against the shore, tossing in a rapid, going deep and still in deep pools. We sometimes round a bend to startle a fisherman staring silently at the water as it curls spins and flows on.

As beautiful as the water is, there is something haunting in it. As we drift down the first miles of the canyon, I notice gray driftlogs lodged in cracks 20 feet above the canoe, and the cliffs wear the unmistakable chalk-white streak of a waterline higher than I could reach standing in the boat.

These are the signs of a power in the river that seems to rival the power in the rocks. The Gunnison River flows through what geologists call the oldest valley in Colorado. It is gathered among peaks 14,000 feet high and, with the slow grace of water, has cut a canyon deep into bedrock, rock that makes up what writer Doug Wheat has called "the sleeping roots of the Ancestral Rocky Mountains."

The same water that strings around my paddle like clear strands of smoke, softly carries a strength almost beyond comprehension: snowflakes that cut through rock. To look into the deep black eyes of the Gunnison Gorge and the clear river that flows through its heart is to have your concept of power forever shattered.

Beneath the canoe, dancing like shadows through the light of a prism, trout play in the pools. This is trout water, Gold Medal Trout water, the kind of place that can make trout bums get up in the middle of a hard winter's night to tie flies. Those shadows deep in the pools of cold, green water make the Gunnison Gorge a fisherman's dream. Twenty-six miles of the river have been officially designated a Gold Medal Trout fishery. That same 26 miles, including the section in the Black Canyon and the Gorge, have been recommended for inclusion in the National Wild and Scenic Rivers System. When that green water is tossed and turned white, the river becomes another sort of dream: a paddler's dream. The first miles flow easily through the Gunnison Gorge, through the small Improvise Rapid and Upper Pucker. We are taking the 14 miles of river and turning it into a two-day trip and so our pace is slow. Our paddles rarely touch the water, our eyes on the canyon walls as much as on the river.

Then, just above the Boulder Garden, the walls of the canyon seem to clench like a fist, closing in on the river. One minute there is calm water and a wide river, the next a sidecanyon has pinched the river nearly in half. It is a sign. From here the river drops off more sharply, the gradient increasing to 43 feet per mile, speeding up, shedding its tameness. An acceleration can be felt under the canoe like a gust of wind, but we fight it, pull over and make camp just above the rapid.

Our trip is at a time long before the official maps of the area have been made, at a time when we know no official names for any of the rapids or rock formations. Without the names, there seems a kind of innocence about the place. It seems wilder. Around the fire that night we talk about names for the rapids, even suggesting a few, but then leave it at that, knowing that the best and most respectful way is to leave them nameless. Just as we are crawling into our sleeping bags, a full moon breaks over the canyon and lights it like a candle.

When I open my eyes, the sun is where the moon rose last night, pouring sunshine on the canyon walls, while the river and our camp are still deep in shadows. Before breakfast I crawl up the cliffs, aiming for the sunshine. The sound of the rapid fades as I climb. Suddenly, another sound, like the rush of air as when a rock passes the ear. A peregrine falcon slices out of the sidecanyon above camp. It flies straight and fast and directly at eye level from where I stand on the cliff. When it reaches the river corridor, it tilts to find an angle of the wind that will take it downstream. I have watched peregrine falcons for hours on high Arctic rivers and there is no mistaking its barred breast and the sharp curl of its beak. It catches the angle and is gone, leaving only the faint sounds of the river to flow in behind it, now carrying a deeper and wilder tone.

The sight of a peregrine falcon on the wing, like the sound of wolves howling, is a sign of a pure and untamed place. It is a sign of how this one last stretch of the Gunnison River is fighting to stay wild. On the climb down, I feel my hands searching the rocks for angles as if in wind.

The sound of the rapid grows as I climb down. What the falcon flew over, we will have to paddle through—a jumbled collection of boulders which have tumbled to the river from the sidecanyon. By bigwater standards it is not much. The difficulty lies in the tight maneuvering that must be done, and without error. Technical, I suppose the guidebooks would call it.

With the route committed to memory, Beck and I are in the canoe and on that soft spot found in every rapid just before the drop, a place where the water feels like silk. The first wave tosses us sideways and the noise of the rapid surrounds us. Luckily Beck and I read water the same way and there is no need for shouting directions or instructions. From the stern he seems to anticipate each move I am making in the bow, and we slip through the rocks in the upper rapid as easily as wind through the grass. At the end, a grand finale, there is a sharp right-hand bend around a huge boulder barely wide enough for the canoe, but I reach out and brace as high as I can, a move that Beck anticipates again, and we slide through to the quietwater below.

Two miles below, the rapids seem to grow. We spend a long time looking at the Narrows where the entire river slams into the wall and bounces off for a right-hand turn. A paddleboat will bounce, a canoe won't, and so Beck and I spend a long time looking. There is no need to talk since we read water so much alike. We just look.

Then we run. We put the canoe at an angle to the curve, like an arrow cutting through the wind, hit the big wave so hard my teeth rattle, but before we can worry about rattling teeth, we are both leaning far over and bracing hard and the small pillow wave against the rock pushes us safely away from the wall and back into quietwater. The paddleboat bounces, as paddleboats do, and we continue downstream through other rapids we have no names for, that will later be called The Drops, Cable and Grande Finale.

As if in salute, a final statement, the canyon narrows abruptly just below the last rapid into a short, shadowy hall that seems as wild as any place on the river has ever been. Of the more than 50 miles that once were part of the Black Canyon of the Gunnison, only 26 miles remain. The rest are buried beneath the waters of the Curecanti Project upstream. Drifting through this last narrow passage of what remains, it is impossible not to wonder how the light must have played in those other canyons, how the waters must have sung on those other bends of the river now silenced.

This is the stretch of the Gunnison that still sings. It is a beautiful, stubborn song. For hundreds of thousands of years the river has refused to turn away from the hard rock, carving the oldest canyon in Colorado through solid granite. Even though choked by three dams upstream, it has held on to its beauty in the gorge. It is a difficult river to find, hidden as it is in the deep crack of the gorge. It is a difficult river to reach over the teeth-jarring dirt roads that can turn to mud traps in the rain or vanish in the dust.

But with one look into the deep green waters of the Gunnison River, one solid tug on the end of a fly rod from a shadow in one of the deep holes, one sound of a rapid rumbling just downstream around the bend, the difficulties flow off with the current.

As we drive away from the take-out, the river and its canyon seem to vanish back into the sagebrush and dustclouds like a mirage. The horizon closes in and hardens, looking like an unlikely place for a river with the beauty and wildness of the Gunnison. It is hidden well, those last precious free-flowing miles of the Gunnison River, but there is a river there. Yes, there is a river.

14

KLAMATH RIVER

MAIN RUN

Brian Clark

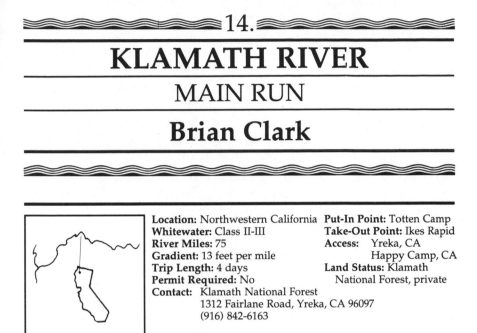

Location: Northwestern California | **Put-In Point:** Totten Camp
Whitewater: Class II-III | **Take-Out Point:** Ikes Rapid
River Miles: 75 | **Access:** Yreka, CA
Gradient: 13 feet per mile | Happy Camp, CA
Trip Length: 4 days | **Land Status:** Klamath
Permit Required: No | National Forest, private
Contact: Klamath National Forest
1312 Fairlane Road, Yreka, CA 96097
(916) 842-6163

We moved quietly out of the eddy and slid into the main current of the river. With a gentle tug, the rolling Klamath River caught our kayaks and pulled us downstream into a flowing ribbon of blue-green water surrounded by tall trees, squat bushes, myriad ferns, shrubs and soaring mountains.

"Shhh," said Shelley, my wife and paddling partner on that late spring day as we floated down a gentle section of the "Klam" as those who love this river call it. This surging stream of rapids and long calm pools on the California/Oregon border is the home to more than 300 species of birds. They range from the fish hawk, known as the osprey, to the minute hummingbird, the leggy blue heron, and the wizard-like owls and proud eagles.

Draining some 4,000 square miles of terrain that includes near-rain forest and high desert, the Klamath begins its journey in Lake

Ewauna in southern Oregon. Unlike its chilly sister rivers in the
Sierras, it doesn't tumble down abruptly from high peaks to the
valley below. It meanders through high valleys and long calm
stretches that allow it to warm up, making it a perfect spot for swimming and teaching kayak lessons. No hypothermia here for a stu-
dent who spends half of his or her time upside-down learning the
Eskimo roll.

From modest beginnings, the Klam cuts through the Cascades
and roars through a rapid-choked gorge known as the Upper
Klamath. Unfortunately, this run is threatened by the Salt Cave Hydroelectric project, which could de-water much of this great run. Below the Iron Gate Reservoir, the river slices through the Coast Range
in northwestern California on the west side of Interstate 5, before
slowing down and mixing with the saltwater of the Pacific Ocean.
This lower section is a Wild and Scenic River, which means it is protected from the dam builders who would quiet its tumbling waters
behind dams, trading its cascades and gurgling riffles for electrical
power to run air conditioners, kitchen appliances and industry.

"Let's not paddle, let's just drift a bit and watch the merganser
family up there," Shelley said. "This is their place too. Let's not
startle them unless we have to."

Often more interested in catching little eddies, surfing big waves
and doing nose stands in reversals, I hadn't been aware of the birds
we were sharing the river with. But for Shelley, a naturalist with
scores of guidebooks on her shelves, the waterfowl had practically
jumped out at her.

Before I could say "What birds?" a group of 10 gray-backed and
light brown merganser chicks and their mother zipped out on the
water from under the limbs of an overhanging tree about 30 feet
away. We had invaded their territory. Taking note that the helmeted
creatures approaching them were 12 feet long and had bright red
and yellow bodies, they gave ground—or in this case, water. Instinc-
tively picking the proper ferry angle—or do mergansers have to
practice as much as human boaters?—the birds scudded across the
stream and moved to the other side, giving us hardly a second
glance.

That was only the beginning. Almost every eddy that we caught
seemed to have a family of mergansers in it. Six here, a dozen there,
10 more down the river. We were shaking our heads at the wealth of
bird life when we rounded a corner and came upon the biggest flock

of all. In the decade I've been rafting and kayaking rivers around the West, I've never seen more than 15 young following a mother merganser. Usually the number is something around a half-dozen. I thought I was seeing double, or even triple, when we came upon a mature female and about 30 young. I blinked, looked again and started counting over. When mama moved left, the flock moved with her. When she moved right, they stepped smartly, acting as if they'd been around her for awhile.

We gave the birds a wide berth and popped into an eddy across the river. Had that merganser made avian medical history? Or had the brood of another female or two simply joined up with this flock? We watched for awhile and then headed downstream in search of more waves, a rapid or two, more eddies and maybe even more birds.

I remembered what the caretaker at the put-in campground had told us earlier that morning. He was a retired logger who had grown up on the Klamath who loved to watch for different birds and keep track of what species he'd seen. Even though the Klamath still seemed rich in wildlife, he said he'd seen even larger flocks of birds when he was a boy, back before high-tech logging practices began denuding large patches of the forest above the river, sending tons of silt into the water. Logging has also threatened habitat for black bear, cougar, bobcat, deer and elk. Years ago, even the grizzly bear roamed the Klamath Valley.

There were once more Indians in the Klamath Basin as well. Before the California gold rush which began at the burg of Coloma on the South Fork of the American River, the Klamath River Valley was home to the Shasta, Karok and Yurok Indians. Though for years whites had penetrated the valley in small numbers looking for beaver and exploring for the Hudson Bay Company, they had never posed much of a threat to the Native Americans.

That all changed when the cry of "Gold!" rang out. Thousands of miners from all corners of the world flooded the hills. The Indians of the Klamath River were shot, died from diseases brought in by the white man, or were driven from their land to far-off reservations.

Miners used a variety of techniques to get to the gold. One of the most destructive used jets of high-pressure water from cannon-like firehoses to wash down whole hillsides to get at flakes of gold buried in the ancient gravel. By the late 1800s, the surface gold, which brought $10 an ounce, was gone. So were the miners. The region turned to small-scale logging and agriculture. Today, with gold at $450 an ounce, miners using small dredges are back on the river using noisy, gas-driven engines to suck up gravel and run it through a sluice. More than a few harsh words have been traded between boaters and miners.

Back on the river, we peeled out into the main current again and came upon a cackling kingfisher looking for its lunch in the river. Then, ever trying to paddle quietly, we spied a great blue heron, a stork-like bird with long spindly legs that looks as if it could be a throwback to the pterodactyl and the age of dinosaurs. It was light blue and showed little fear at our passing. Only when we were 10 feet away did it lift off the tree branch, making its ungainly first flaps and bringing its pencil-thin legs up to its body.

Later that night, we settled in at the Sarah Totten Campground. It was named after the lady who ran a local general store and a hotel that some called a cathouse. Our talk turned once again to birds. As we had driven along the road that day, coming to an osprey nest out-side a small Klamath River town called Hamburg. The osprey and two chicks were in a tall pine far above the river, yet not too distant from the road for good viewing. We got out and watched, trying not to bother the birds. But the female heard the crunching of our shoes on the pine needles and lifted off, squawking loudly. Obviously irri-tated, she circled the nest, then swung off to the north side of the river and dove on a blue heron nest. Not wanting to stir up a neigh-borhood fight, we retreated and the osprey returned to her nest.

More than birds had drawn us north to run the Klamath. There are plenty of action-packed rapids on the river, and we were deter-mined to experience them. In addition to kayaks and inflatable neoprene rafts, dories also ply the Klamath and are especially popular for fishing during the salmon runs. The next day we hooked up with some rafting friends and took on the Hamburg Rapid. It is a Class III affair that has a few large rocks and holes, but also plenty of river that allowed us to skirt the danger spots.

The next day we came to raft-bucking drops like the Upper and Lower Savage rapids, Fort Goff Falls and Otter's Playpen—the latter appropriately named for those impish river dwellers who love to build mud slides and play in and along the river. Devil's Toenail and Rattlesnake Rapids gave us good splashes too. But it wasn't until we got to Ishi Pishi (End of the Trail) Falls above the town of Somes Bar, that our eyes really bugged out. We wisely opted not to run this drop, portaged our boats around and saved our strength for the series of Ikes below.

A boating friend once told me that the first time he heard of the Ikes, he was certain they were named the Yikes. It is a worthy name, for that trio of rapids can appear a bit frightening. After scouting, we ran Little Ike on the left, Ike's Falls from right to left, and then skirted a large boulder and reversal in the middle of Big Ike. They were a delight.

At the bottom of the Ikes, we took our boats out of the water and sat in the shade to say "Cheers" to our days on the Klamath. And we made a special toast to those who had worked to make it a part of the National Wild and Scenic Rivers System.

15

KOBUK RIVER

HEADWATERS RUN

Jeff Rennicke

Location: Northwestern Alaska	**Put-In Point:** Walker Lake
Whitewater: Class II	**Take-Out Point:** Kobuk Village
River Miles: 125	**Access:** Fairbanks, AK
Gradient: 4 feet per mile	**Land Status:** Gates of the Arctic
Trip Length: 12 days	National Park and Preserve
Permit Required: No	
Contact: Gates of the Arctic	
National Park and Preserve	
P.O. Box 74680, Fairbanks, AK 99707	
(907) 456-0281	

Sudden, the way that water flows in behind a stone tossed in the river. The floatplane that dropped me here drones off over the ridge to the southwest and the silence flows back in suddenly. I am alone in the Arctic, solo.

I have forgotten the silence; I always do. It is like a bird song just on the edge of hearing and too sweet and sad to be remembered fully. Even with the grizzlies, the caribou and the wolf, one of Alaska's greatest natural resources is its silence. Here, it is as much a part of the landscape as wind or rock.

And I come into it gladly. I have come to this place to hear the silence again. Too many months in the city with its groundswell of noise, too long away from a silence so deep you can hear the river. It has been years since I've heard a river flow unbroken for days. So I've come here, to the headwaters to start again.

In all the years I've been running rivers in North America, I can count on one hand the number of trips that began at the beginning, the headwaters. Most trips begin wherever the first road happens to nudge up against the river, at the most convenient place and surrounded by sheet metal outhouses and signboards leafed in regulation forms. Running only sections of a river is like listening to scattered notes ripped from a song. This time, I want to hear the whole tune. There is a single caribou splashing in the water along the shore—once, twice and then falls silent.

The river begins where that first tug of current pulls my kayak out of Walker Lake. I paddle once, hard, and stop. The kayak catches the current and drifts. The Kobuk River is born. Below, a school of grayling has gathered to feed at the outlet. In the clear water, they are as bright as polished stones.

I can't help thinking of the way the pilot shook my hand twice and with a little too much ceremony, as if he never planned on seeing me again. "Solo," he kept saying, shaking his head like he had water in his ear. I smile at the thought of him flying now somewhere over the ridge still shaking his head.

Drifting quietly, listening for the roar of the rapid we scouted from the plane, I round a bend to find a cow moose with triplet calves feeding at mid-stream. The young calves, soaked from the river and glistening in the sun, are the color of polished wood and have not yet mastered the workings of their long, spindly legs. Twice, one of the calves founders as the cow leads them out of the river. As the bow of my kayak touches shore for the scout, the moose vanish into the brush. There are grizzly tracks in the wet sand.

The Upper Kobuk Canyon rapid is just a flexing of the river's muscle, really—a short stretch of small ripples that cuts left and builds into some wild Class III drops and holes. Standing above it on a rock, there is no clear route to be seen. Several of the holes look ragged enough to be trouble, but the tailwaves look inviting. Still, I am solo and every solo trip, no matter how many times you've paddled the river, is a first descent. So I compromise, portaging the gut of the rapid and riding out the tailwaves below, playing once in a wave that pulses as if with a heartbeat.

Turning out of the hole finally, I pass a rock with a snapped kayak paddle jammed in a crack, its edges ragged as a broken bone. Suddenly the water seems colder and the rocks sharper and the decision to portage a little wiser.

The motion of the river against its banks seems almost hyp-notic—the sun, the soft sounds of water, the silence as I sit still as stone listening for my own heartbeat. The silence washes over me like wind. I lay the paddle across the bow, lean back and drift, alone.

Suddenly, I am not alone. A wolf slides over a cutbank on the left shore, steps to the river and drinks. Its fur is a tangle of gray streaked with silver, the color of summer storm clouds. As it steps to the river's edge its reflection rises from the still water to meet it. I paddle once to turn the bow and then freeze, watching.

It looks up once, puzzled, looking directly at me. The kayak drifts to within 20 yards. The wolf turns and trots downstream at about the speed of the river. I drift closer: 15 yards. The animal moves with the grace of water, smooth and supple. I can see the muscles strapped across its back rippling beneath its thin summer fur with each step. As it crosses a broad, flat rock, I hear the cut of its claws against the stone. I drift closer: 10 yards. It stops to check a scent at a driftlog. A bolt of sunlight flashes off my paddle and the wolf is gone. Just like that, I am alone again.

This far north the sun never sets in summer; the days flow together as easily as creeks come to the river and give time a feeling of endlessness, of suspension. All the signs are here; the shadows grow long, the air goes still and cool, the light gets heavy and the nightbirds call, but the sun just circles the sky endlessly like a wanderer looking for a home. I give in to its lack of rhythm, paddling when the weather is good or when I feel a restlessness, sitting for hours on the bank memorizing cloud patterns or looking for pieces of local jade on the gravel bars. I paddle most when the sun is low; late in the day when I, like the sun, am looking for a place to rest.

It is on one of these late-night paddles, under light the color of honey, that I come into the Lower Kobuk Canyon. From out of nowhere black walls rise up like a fist closing on the river and the air hums with the sound of rapids. An osprey is circling overhead. Its sharp call slices through even the roar of the rapids.

This is what I've come for, a dream-like run, playing alone in the holes with no rush to move on, no designated campsites. Only the flow of the river, the light that turns the waves to splashes of diamonds as my paddle flashes through. In light and water, there is a common bond and, in between, there is a single, solo kayak playing, forever playing. The osprey is still circling overhead, call-ing. There is a light in its feathers like lightning.

I awake with a start. A raven just overhead makes a sound like cracking rock and then flaps off downstream. I have fallen asleep in a quiet patch of cottonwood on a hillside overlooking the confluence of the Pah and the Kobuk. There, among the shadows from the trees, are a pair of weather-beaten shacks, shoulder high and quiet: Eskimo grave huts. The wind in the leaves sounds like distant voices.

There is a perception of Alaska as being an unbroken and unbreakable wilderness, endless. Some of it still is, but much of this land carries a long human history, a history that has not always left tracks any deeper than footprints on a riverbank or the split branches of spruce used as a tent frame, but a history just the same.

Archaeologists believe that the Kobuk Valley may have been the gateway to this continent for nomadic hunters crossing the Bering Land Bridge. Downstream, at Onion Portage, is one of the oldest known sites of human habitation in North America.

The people at the villages downstream—Kobuk, Shugnak, Ambler—know this river as intimately as the pattern of beads sewn on their winter parkas. I drift past their fish camps, abandoned until the fall salmon runs, the split spruce drying racks stained dark with the blood of generations of salmon. The village of Kobuk is nothing but a cluster of government houses and a few old log cabins overlooking the right bank of the river, two small stores and an immense post office painted bright red and sporting a huge radio dish out back next to a skin-drying rack. A gravel runway, the only way in or out of town besides the river, cuts just behind the post office. At the sound of each plane, children gather to write notes in the dust on the belly of the plane to be read by the children of the next isolated village.

As I wait for the plane, I cut up salmon with an old woman on the shore. Her hands seem as bent and dark as slabs of driftwood, yet she handles her *ulu*, the traditional Eskimo rounded knife, with grace and speed, cutting two fish for each one of mine. A long time ago, she tells me, she paddled the Kobuk in an *umiak*, a skin kayak, and she makes a paddling motion with her hands, throwing her head back in laughter. "Now, my fat would sink the boat," she laughs, a dry, soft sound like sticks cracking.

We cut on in silence for more than a half-hour until finally she asks, "Did you paddle all alone?" I hesitate, thinking of the broken kayak paddle, of the wolf, of the grave huts where the trees talk in quiet voices, and of the people who for thousands of years have cut up salmon just like this on the banks of this river. For just a moment, staring into her ancient eyes, I am not quite sure how to answer.

THE OWYHEE RIVER

THREE FORKS TO ROME

Paul Hoobyar

≈≈≈≈≈≈≈≈≈≈≈≈≈≈≈≈≈≈≈≈≈≈≈≈≈

Location: Southeastern Oregon	**Put-In Point:** Three Forks
Whitewater: Class III-IV	**Take Out Point:** Rome
River Miles: 32	**Access:** Rome, OR
Gradient: 22 feet per mile	**Land Status:** State Scenic
Trip Length: 3 to 5 days	Waterway, National Wild and
Permit Required: Yes	Scenic Rivers System

Contact: Bureau of Land Management
Vale District Office
P.O. 700
Vale, OR 97918

Driving east through southern Oregon you leave the snow-capped majesty of the Cascade Mountains and enter a desert country of broad plateaus, sagebrush and distant, stark mountains. Towns with names like Alkali Lake and Wagontire bake under an unforgiving sun next to the highway. The typical business district consists of a spindly gas pump in front of a small general store, its screen door skewed and rattling in the wind. A handful of mobile homes shaped like burnt aluminum hotdog buns litter the town's peripheries. One of the least populated regions in the continental United States, this area has an average rainfall of less than 10 inches a year.

This is also the access to the Owhyee River in southeastern Oregon. The classic, sun-bleached cattle skulls dotting the unpopulated expanses make it obvious this river runs through remote and rugged country.

We had hoped to get on the water by mid-day after we left the town of Rome some 50 miles before, but the 30-plus miles of dirt road leading from Highway 95 to the Owyhee River canyon were not user-friendly to our van. Two tire ruts with a high ridge between them defined the road. As we came to the top of each rise we could see the two beige ribbons stretching for miles across the desert in front of us. Our rig splashed through raft-sized mud holes and yards of fresh cow pies. The mud and manure dried instantly on the sides of the trailered bottom boat, texturing the boat like a plasterer finishing the walls of a room.

Finally we came over a rise and looked down at the confluence of the east, north and south forks of the Owyhee Rivers. Sheer cliffs rose abruptly from the water above the confluence, giving me a forlorn, desolate feeling as I looked at them. The river ran brown below the confluence before it snaked around a bend and disappeared.

The road worsened as we made our final descent to the river, and by the time we got our two rafts, two drift boats and two kayaks ready, it was half past two. But it was the middle of May and we figured there was plenty of light yet, so we headed downstream.

I decided to take my wooden drift boat on the trip, even though most everyone I talked to said the Three Forks section was too difficult a trip for drift boats. I had been testing my limits with the boat, running some tough Oregon rivers: the Illinois, the North Fork of the Umpqua at high water and the upper McKenzie. I felt ready for a new challenge. I had heard that the Three Forks to Rome stretch of the Owyhee was more difficult than the Illinois for a drift boat and I wanted to find out if that was true. Plus, if we decided to run the lower section below Rome, a drift boat would make the perfect craft.

Stiff headwinds greeted us as we got on the water. Our trip started with relatively easy Class II and Class III water. One of the first things I noticed was how hard it was to determine where the rocks were in the muddy brown fluid. My oars clacked and bumped on rocks as I dipped them in the rapids.

About a mile and a half downstream from the put-in lies the first gut-wrencher on this section. Called the Ledge Rapid, this Class IV drop gets its name from a weird pour-over near the head of the rapid. The main rapid has a Class II preamble leading into it and a long Class III+ boulder garden below it. The entire rapid looks almost a half-mile long. Boulders and rocks clutter the river like commuter traffic on the Santa Ana Freeway at five o'clock. As I scouted from the left bank I knew the key to having a good run was keeping track of all the marker rocks so I wouldn't get lost in the middle of the rapid. I slowly walked upstream back to my boat, continually checking my marker rocks to make sure I knew their shape and position as I entered the rapid.

This section of the Owhyee runs through a steep canyon of coarse basalt, and as I slipped into the top of the rapid I kept noticing the abrasive surfaces of the rocks. "Can't look at them now," I told myself, "got to keep track of how to pick my way through this maze."

As the river gained speed at the Ledge, I slowed the boat down, positioned her at the lip and spilled over the pour-off exactly where I needed to be. The rock maze downstream of the pour-off kept me busy, but the boat nosed her way around the rocks like a dog going down a back alley littered with garbage cans.

The strong headwinds continued up the canyon, and the late afternoon sun turned the cliffs and spires on the north side of the river into orange painted murals. "So this is the Owyhee," I thought. The tall spires, wind-carved turrets and sheer canyon walls created a remote, exotic feeling unlike any other river I had experienced in the Pacific Northwest.

The name Owyhee comes from the common spelling for Hawaii at the turn of the 19th century. Islanders, as Hawaiians were called then, worked as laborers and helped establish forts and trading posts in the wilderness of the Pacific Northwest. In 1819, two Hawaiians were part of a hunting party from Fort Okanagan on the Columbia River. The party encountered a band of Native Americans not far from the river, and the two Hawaiians were killed, hence the name.

This desert canyon is so far removed from anything I had experienced in Hawaii, except the lava fields of Kilauea Crater, that I chuckled to think this arid, rock-walled bake oven was named for people who live in a tropical paradise. The river has its own beauty, but it is a beauty derived from conditions at the opposite end of the meteorological spectrum from Hawaii.

We camped about a mile downstream of Ledge Rapid in front of an abandoned cabin. After breakfast, we poked around the cabin and found an ancient wheelbarrow. Its wheel still turned and its handles were still intact, and the dry air had left the metal virtually rust-free. The lifestyle the builder of that cabin must have had in the remote, harsh canyon couldn't have been fun, but if it was solitude he was after, he was paid well.

Once on the water, we passed other cabins and ruins left by early homesteaders. The river ambled along with long flat pools and easy Class II rapids. While we enjoyed our relaxed pace and easy drift, my mind raced ahead to the inevitable loss of gradient that had to be waiting some place downstream.

About six miles below camp the river silted in a dirty white froth around a bend and ran from a Class II drop right into a nasty Class IV+ rapid called Halfmile. Again, I found myself walking up and down the bank, looking at the mandatory chutes and marker rocks, trying to fix a grid sheet in my mind of where I needed to be at each phase of the run.

Halfmile Rapid has two distinct sections in it. The first part of the rapid was straightforward enough, but it funnelled the main current into a riffraff of rocks and debris below. The trick was going to be in running the upper section with enough control to be in good position to miss the hard rocks below. Knowing that the currents would be a lot more powerful than they looked from the bank, I worried about how to get my boat in good position.

I danced through the Class II opener and dropped through the big waves without shipping a lot of water in the upper section of Halfmile. As the jumble of rocks and confusion came into view, I kicked my stern over and began frantically ferrying left to miss the rock pile receiving the brunt of the river's fury. I stroked my cookies off, but the water pushed my boat toward that rock like a toddler lurching toward a lollipop in an outstretched hand. I couldn't pull away from that reef of rocks, and in the last sickening moment I watched as wood and rock united. Those basalt rocks had teeth in them. They chewed through my chine and broke it next to the passenger seat with a crunch that made my stomach sick. Earl, my partner up front, put his foot over the dented oak chine and pushed it back into shape as water sprayed through the crack.

With a little duct tape, and a few more deft kicks with Earl's foot, the boat was ready to press on downstream—probably more ready than I was at that moment. We portaged part of the next rapid and had three more tough drops ahead of us in the next five miles.

At Raftflip Rapid, the river drops into a deep hole in the middle of the channel. My line was to clip the river-left side of the hole, but we ended up out in the middle with the reversing wave breaking over the bow and drenching both Earl and me. The water came in with such force that it knocked the fly deck out of the bow of the boat.

Earl turned around and gazed at me with that "What the hell are you doing?" look about him. What could I say? My boating was off.

We ran the final two heavies in good order. The second rapid is called Bombshelter Drop, after, I assume, the cave just downstream of the rapid. I, for one, was ready to camp, and I think everyone was ready to get off that ditch. We camped on the beach in front of the cave.

A half-moon rose above the high-banked wall behind camp and cast a silver patina on the rock faces and tall spires across the river. The soft contrasts of shadows and light got every shutterbug on the trip trying to capture the scene on film. Watching Earl lie on his back in a prone yoga-like position, supporting his camera with the aid of rocks, made me glad I forgot to bring my camera on the trip.

In the two days we had been on the water, we saw only one other party—an added bonus on a remote, short-season river like the Owyhee. The solitude worked on us in favorable ways, letting us relax and mosey downstream at whatever pace we felt like. It's rare to find a river in the lower 48 so devoid of other boaters.

The river took on a sinister look the next day as it poured through a series of Class III+ and Class IV runs ending in the Class V+ falls of Widowmaker Rapid. We all walked the entire length of the rapid, including the fairly easy opening set, to see just how far we could boat the series. The rafters and kayakers looked at the entire series of rapids with an eye to running it. Stich, the other drift boater, and I looked at it with an eye to minimize our portage.

Stich and I ran our boats down to the lip of Widowmaker's major hydraulics, then tied off our boats to watch the rafters. Both rafts ran the center-left side of Widowmaker, tucking behind a big knifeblade of rock above the major falls and coaxing their rigs over a ramp of water flushing past 18-wheeler-sized holes on either side.

Portaging Widowmaker was the worst portage I've ever done in my life. It was a good thing all the members of our group were close friends, because there was a lot of bitching as we packed two 300-plus pound drift boats around and over the house-sized boulders on the right riverbank.

At one point we were so far above the river, and the group was bitching about the portage so much, that I had visions of everyone walking away and leaving me stranded there with the drift boat. People would pass by in future years and find a blistered, sun-baked drift boat 100 feet above Widowmaker Rapid with a mummified human carcass in it and wonder how the old boy made it that far before he stalled out.

Below Widowmaker, the river drops through a number of Class III and Class III+ rapids for the rest of the run. Campsites become scarce about five miles below Widowmaker, so we decided to camp while there were plenty of good beaches and benches along the right riverbank.

The final stretch of the run is tame enough to allow long looks at the canyon and the countryside. It was a welcome break from the intensity upstream. As we stacked Stich's drift boat on the trailer at the take-out, some of the fresh cow pies that had splattered his boat on the way into Three Forks still clung to his boat after all that hairball whitewater. Stitch had his memento of the trip, and looking at the rent in my boat from Halfmile Rapid, I had mine.

17

RIO CHAMA

CHAMA CANYON

Verne Huser

Location: Northwestern New Mexico
Whitewater: Class II   **Put-In Point:** El Vado Ranch
River Miles: 33   **Take-Out Point:** Forest Road 151
Gradient: 15 feet per mile   **Access:** Tierra Amarillo, NM
Trip Length: 2 days   **Land Status:** BLM, private
Permit Required: Not at present
                    (will be required by 1989)
Contact: Bureau of Land Management
              P.O. Box 1045, Taos, NM 87571
              (505) 758-8851

In the land where Pueblo Indian and Hispanic cultures have mixed for years, they call it El Rio Chama. It is a mild-natured, gentle river, a quiet stream flowing through a forested canyon, a remnant of the bucolic setting of northwestern New Mexico.

The Rio Chama, a tributary of the better-known Rio Grande, is New Mexico's only river to be given protective designation at the state level. The Rio Grande is in part protected as one of the original eight wild rivers in the National Wild and Scenic Rivers System created in 1968. Both are high-desert rivers that originate in Colorado and flow into New Mexico, but there the similarity ends.

The Chama runs in leisurely fashion through a wide canyon of pastoral hues, full of light reminiscent of a Swinnerton painting. The Rio Grande roars through a narrow gorge of dark basalt, as harsh and foreboding as a scene from Dante. While the Rio Chama is best

102

known for its gentle flow, its family-floating flavor, and its good fishing and scenic beauty, the Rio Grande is known for its wild whitewater and for the danger of its rapids and bridges.

Flowing unfettered through northern New Mexico's basaltic plain, the Rio Grande is normally run only by experienced rafters and kayakers. The Rio Chama, marred by two dams and the slack-water reservoirs they impound, is commonly canoed and is also popular with novice rafters and beginning kayakers, as well as with "sportyakers." Only one significant rapid marks its canyon course, though there are a number of rock gardens.

A roughly 30-mile stretch of the Rio Chama between El Vado Dam and Abiquiu Reservoir was designated by the New Mexico State Legislature in 1977 as the state's first (and to date only) Scenic and Pastoral River, to provide "preservation, protection and maintenance of the natural and scenic beauty" of the middle of the Chama. This is the country best known through the paintings of Georgia O'Keefe. It is the land of Ghost Ranch, of rural Hispanic communities and of ancient Indian cultures.

In fact, the very name *Chama* is thought to derive from an ancient Tewa Indian word "*tzama*," meaning "here they have wrestled." And the wrestling continues today over the protected segment of the Chama. In the spring of 1985, when unprecedented high waters filled the rivers and reservoirs of northern New Mexico, Abiquiu Reservoir was raised beyond its legal capacity, an action that inundated private lands, archaeological sites, bald eagle roosting trees and a portion of the "protected" river. It turned the traditional take-out at Adobe Ruins to ugly mud flats. When the State of New Mexico sued the Army Corps of Engineers over the matter, the federal agency began studying the feasibility of increasing the capacity of Abiquiu Reservoir four-fold, which would drown the lower four miles of the Scenic and Pastoral Chama and inundate many of the best rapids. Federal law, and the Army Corps of Engineers, ignored the will of the people and the New Mexico State Legislature.

A group known as the Rio Chama Preservation Trust has emerged to wrestle with the Army, the federal government and whatever other interests would destroy (or inundate) the protected Chama. Trust directors include state officials, local land owners, environmental groups, agricultural interests and recreationists.

The trust even has Reaganomics on its side: no more free lunches or free water storage. Water users who want to store water in federally owned or operated facilities now have to pay their fair share, which amounts to some $20 per acre foot per year, a bit high for traditional uses in New Mexico.

The protected 30-mile stretch of the Rio Chama can readily be divided into two segments: the upper 20-plus miles of unroaded river flowing through the broad pastel canyon, and the lower 10 miles along the road to Christ in the Desert Monastery. Most of the rapids lie below the monastery.

The canyon segment is one of my favorite rivers. It is a get-away river where the fishing is good—native trout, rainbows and browns —and the living is easy. Native grasses line the shoreline, which fluctuates with the reservoir releases and thunderstorm activity. In a wet year, wildflowers are in the greatest abundance and variety I have seen on any river.

Wildlife that call the canyon home include deer, beaver, raccoon, coyote, even bear and cougar. Birds are abundant and variable, everything from sandhill cranes heading for the Bosque de Apache National Wildlife Refuge (with their surrogate whooping crane offspring) to an amazing range of raptors, shorebirds, waterfowl and passerines found in riparian habitat, including the rare blue grosbeak.

Spring is the primary river-running season in New Mexico as snowmelt fills the streams, and early summer is the rainy season with daily thunderstorms common. By the Fourth of July, the Chama is normally too low to run, but since downstream irrigators need the water stored in El Vado Reservoir, carefully coordinated releases can serve both the agricultural interests and river runners. Through the efforts of the New Mexico Department of Natural Resources, with the cooperation of the City of Albuquerque and the Middle Rio Grande Conservancy District, the Rio Chama had runnable water levels on two long weekends during the summer of 1986.

On both the July Fourth and Labor Day weekends there were mobs of floaters at the put-in at the privately owned El Vado Ranch immediately below the dam. Once on the river, however, the mobs seemed to disappear into the landscape. We rarely saw another party, had no trouble finding perfect campsites and enjoyed the solitude of wilderness. On one two-day trip, our seven-person party traveled in a 13-foot raft and a sportyak; on the other, nine of us used the same raft and a 16-foot canoe.

The river was silty, flowing swiftly at a gradient of about 15 feet per mile. There were few hazards at the 1000 cubic feet per second reservoir-release flow. There were a few big rocks to miss, a few minor sweepers, but generally the run was without difficulty until we reached Chama Number One on the second day, about 12 miles from our launch site. The only major rapid in the canyon is a Class II swing rapid (S-shaped) that drops to the left then turns sharply to the right along a cliff. Rock gardens appear here and there below Chama Number One, but we were able to negotiate them with no problem.

We saw signs of beaver—fresh-cut stumps, peeled sticks and tracks—but no beaver. We found the remains of fish, trapped in backwater ponds by thunderstorm-created flashfloods and then eaten by raccoons, whose tracks were everywhere. There were deer tracks and coyote tracks, the voice of the coyote in the dusky hours, and rabbits and squirrels in abundance.

The birdlife we witnessed was amazing: mountain bluebirds, western tanagers, Townsend's solitaires, Clark's nutcrackers, Stellar's jays and raucous ravens of the high-country forest mixed with ospreys, great blue herons, spotted sandpipers, swallows, swifts, warblers and kingfishers of the riparian habitat as well as the hawks, owls, sparrows, towhees and hummingbirds of the desert.

We saw tall, isolated ponderosa pines on the skyline and dark Douglas fir high in the shady alcoves of the canyon walls. Closer to the river were the symmetrically formed junipers, shaggy piñon pines, ancient gnarled cottonwoods, box elders and even a few oaks, though we found none near our campsites for firewood.

Near the end of the canyon run, the cliffs squeezed in, approaching the river for the first time. Then the river quieted and ran past the monastery in a channelized stretch of placid water that seemed to respect the monks' desire for silence and solitude. The road that parallels the river in the lower 10 miles is the access to the monastery as well as to numerous possible take-out and launch sites and good camping areas.

The lower 10 miles below the monastery offer the best whitewater on the middle Chama, a series of Class II rock gardens and chutes, one of which drops over a tricky ledge. But these can be easily negotiated by canoes and sportyaks operated by experienced paddlers and rowers. Beginning kayakers and rafters in paddleboats love these lower miles of fastwater alternating with slow, meandering loops.

On one of our trips on this lower segment, we lolled on a sandbar for an hour or more waiting for the reservoir release to give us enough water to float on. The schedule for weekend releases was usually from six in the morning until six at night, which meant that 20 miles from the dam you might have to wait seven or eight hours for the rise. You soon learned to calculate the time it takes the water to reach a given point—as you do in the Grand Canyon. That day the surge hit us at half past two in the afternoon.

I like to spend Easter on a river. Twice it's been the Colorado in the Grand Canyon. Once it was the Salmon in Idaho's great central wilderness. Frequently it has been the Snake in the Jackson Hole country of northwest Wyoming. This year it was the Rio Chama.

Weather was superb—warm sunny days with clear frosty nights —and we had the river to ourselves, but for a couple of canoeing turkey hunters and a trio of Colorado guides in a pair of rafts. We saw wild turkeys, the first I have ever spotted from a raft. A golden eagle rose from a grassy bar where we stopped for lunch one day— he'd been feeding on a duck whose feathers littered our lunch area. We even saw a Canada goose stretched out and sunning on a flat riverside rock like something dead—but it was very much alive as it ran along the surface of the water, honking into flight.

Climbing above camp early one morning, I broke through a band of cliffs to find bear tracks in the dried earth—the largest tracks I have ever seen. Though I never saw the animal, it must have been huge, judging from the size and impact of its footsteps. I followed them to a promontory overlooking the river, my own destination. I had intended to survey the river downstream from here; who knows what the bear's purpose might have been?

A herd of five mule deer fleetingly showed themselves as they topped a ridge and disappeared down the other side. Signs of beaver were plentiful throughout our trip, but we saw none of the nocturnal rodents, though we searched the twilight riverbank each evening.

It was a peaceful trip, a quiet trip, an ideal Easter weekend. We ate well, slept late, hiked or fished or loafed on the shore as our moods and personalities dictated.

It is these lower miles of the Rio Chama that are threatened by the proposal to raise the reservoir behind Abiquiu Dam. Downstream irrigators want their water stored as far upstream as possible because evaporation rates are lower in the higher, cooler country. On the other hand, if reservoirs are full of last year's stored water, there is no room for flood control storage, one of the primary justifications for building the dams in the first place.

Much of the water that flows in the Rio Chama has been taken from the San Juan watershed through a federally funded trans-basin diversion known as the San Juan—Chama Project. The water is "owned" by farmers and ranchers who make the river flow when they demand water for irrigation. Normally, releases are not coordinated with the interest or needs of fisheries, wildlife, recreation or other agriculture.

In fact, many of the water users along the Rio Chama are upset with the flood-level demands by downstream irrigators because such sudden high-level surges destroy their simple diversion structures. There is, however, a growing interest in developing a dialogue among the numerous interests that use the Rio Chama—an effort to manage the river in a more logical and equitable fashion.

There is also a move, initiated by the Rio Chama Preservation Trust, to give this segment of the river federal protection as part of the National Wild and Scenic Rivers System, to prevent the Army Corps of Engineers or anyone else from destroying this river. There is strong support for such protective designation.

Already recognized within New Mexico as a scenic and pastoral river, the Rio Chama is a special favorite, not for its mild whitewater but for its placid beauty. The access road to the take-out may be the most challenging aspect of a trip on its silt-laden waters, especially after a good rain. It has none of the macho reputation of the nearby Rio Grande, but it is recommended to anyone who loves the natural world, at almost any time of the year.

Every time I return to the Rio Chama I want it protected, so that it will remain as I have known it for the enjoyment of future generations. We have too few of these rejuvenating resources left, and we need all we can get.

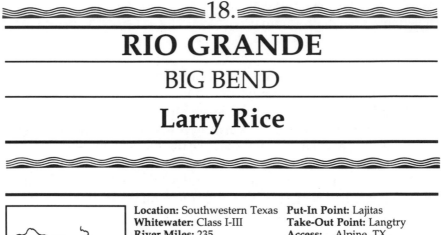

18.

RIO GRANDE

BIG BEND

Larry Rice

Location: Southwestern Texas **Put-In Point:** Lajitas
Whitewater: Class I-III **Take-Out Point:** Langtry
River Miles: 235 **Access:** Alpine, TX
Gradient: 7 feet per mile Marathon, TX
Trip Length: 14 to 21 days **Land Status:** Big Bend National
Permit Required: Yes Park, private, Mexico
Contact: National Park Service,
Big Bend National Park, TX 79834
(915) 477-2251

"Hey, time to get up!" I heard Ron say. I slowly opened my eyes and glanced at my watch. Ugh! Only five o'clock. There's always one weirdo on a river trip who likes to get an early start.

I pulled back my hood and looked around. A cold, faint starlight provided just enough illumination to see my companions still stretched out in sleeping bags on the sandbar nearby. Fred, Don and Louis didn't appreciate the wake-up call either. In a few minutes, the once peaceful Rio Grande canyon erupted in yawns and groans. As if to reply, two great horned owls added to the racket with a few hoots of their own.

I pumped my arms back and forth to warm up. Although the first week of the trip had been sunny and mostly pleasant, the ice in our water bottles reminded us it was still winter.

It was eerie getting our gear together by the light of the head-

108

lamps' darting beams. Bats flickered past and a sheer cliff face, dark and foreboding, loomed overhead. I couldn't make out the river yet, but its endless gurgles and boils were music to my ears. Once we pushed off, the Rio Grande would own us. There would be no turning back, no roads to walk out on, no one to help in case of accident. The 130-mile section of the Rio Grande del Norte, from the eastern edge of Big Bend National Park to Langtry, Texas, is, according to one writer, "probably more isolated than any waterway outside of Alaska in the United States." I was ready for first light, ready for the wild and winding canyons that lay ahead.

Our journey started on Christmas Day at the sleepy town of Lajitas, a few miles outside the park's western boundary. Here we loaded two weeks of gear into two canoes and a kayak for the 250-mile journey downstream.

The first 112 miles of river took us through the spectacular canyons and desert wilderness adjacent to Big Bend. Santa Elena Canyon, 17 miles long, more than a thousand feet deep and oftentimes barely an arm's width wide, was the first major gorge we encountered. Its notorious Rockslide, a jumble of giant boulders clogging the river's flow, lay just inside the canyon's mouth. This is the spot Robert Hill, with the U.S. Geological Survey, called "Camp Misery" in 1899. Hill and his party, on a mapping expedition down the Rio Grande, spent three days portaging around the Rockslide with 300-pound boats and a ton of scientific gear. Over the years, more than one life and one craft had been lost at these rapids, so while Louie kayaked through, the rest of us followed Hill's lead and lined the canoes safely from shore.

A 50-mile stretch of flat, easy-going river led us to the next major gorge. The appearance of seven-mile-long Mariscal Canyon, rising dramatically from the desert plains, brought the dreary landscape to an end. Except for the Rockpile and Tight Squeeze, two obstacles that demand caution, Mariscal can be enjoyed without worrying about a thing, leaving river runners plenty of time to enjoy the scenery between the tightly spaced 1,800-foot walls.

We navigated a few smaller chasms before reaching the final major canyon that separates Mexico from the park. Boquillas Canyon, like Santa Elena, is 17 miles long, but that's where the similarities end. Wide and airy, it is crossed by a number of major sidecanyons, each one begging to be explored. For anyone interested in easy cruising, this is the ideal place to lean back in the boat and unwind.

Stillwell Crossing, eight miles downstream of Boquillas, is the customary take-out for Rio Grande runners. From this point on, the river grows exceedingly remote and is paddled by only a few people each year.

Before entering the lower canyons, we reviewed what Bob Burleson, former president of the Texas Explorers Club, had written about this 130-mile section: "There are many tough rapids, some of which require a portage, and is almost a continuous canyon for three-fourths of the trip. This trip is for properly prepared and experienced river runners, and could be a very arduous and miserable trip for the careless or ignorant adventurer."

Another member of the Texas Explorers summed up a journey from Stillwell Crossing to Langtry this way: "I have often thought of the bad situation which could result if someone broke a leg. There would be no other way to get an injured person out other than to float out over a period of several days. It would be extremely difficult to float an injured person out in a canoe without capsizing several times. The discomfort attendant upon being thrown into the rapids with a crudely splinted broken leg can hardly be described. For this reason I give strict instructions to the members of our expeditions before leaving—"DON'T BREAK NO LEGS!"

With thoughts of doom and destruction swirling through our heads, we pushed off from the sandy bank and were grabbed by the strong current. A short time later we were flushed into what was the first of many canyons to come. Horse Canyon, short and deep, serves as the gateway into the wilderness lying downstream. Rather than risk the heavily laden canoes through the scattered, uncharted rapids, we let Louie go first, in the kayak. When he bobbed safely through the Class II's, the rest of our tiny flotilla followed suit.

We reached Maravillas Creek at mid-day. This usually dry streambed entering from the Texas side marked the last place to leave the river for the next four days, unless we wanted to bushwhack 20 miles across the desert to reach a lonely dirt road. We told Fred, who had been talking constantly about how much he missed his wife, that his opportunity had come to show his devotion by hiking out. Gazing over the barren countryside, he shook his head. "Naw, I think I can handle another week before seeing her again."

We made camp that evening on a broad white sandbar on the Mexican side. A long day of paddling against a cold wind made us ravenous for dinner and a chance to relax, but the temptation to climb one of the nearby hillsides was too great to resist. Trading boat shoes for hiking boots, we headed up the mountain to get an overview of the surrounding land.

The climb to a thousand feet left us breathless and took longer than expected, but the view from above was superb. The Rio Grande appeared pencil thin from our perch. Coffee-colored from wall to wall, the river turned in S-shaped loops and curves before disappearing into hidden canyons far beyond.

The only green in the landscape below existed along the river's banks. Here grew impenetrable thickets of salt cedar, mesquite, seep willow and wild cane. Away from the river was quite a different picture—sparsely covered mountainsides and flats. We were paddling through one of the driest regions in North America and it definitely showed. Typical Chihuahuan Desert plants—creosote, yucca, ocotillo, lechuguilla and several varieties of cacti—coated the land with dull yellows and somber browns.

At first glance this didn't seem to be the kind of country where a person would expect to see much wildlife. But like so many things here, first looks are deceiving. More than 380 species of birds and 75 species of mammals have been seen and recorded in Big Bend National Park. Most of these animals spend part of their time down near the river. We had already spotted mule deer, javelina, coyotes, beavers, great blue herons, ducks, hummingbirds and golden eagles. If we were really lucky, we might observe some of the rarer critters like peregrine falcons, mountain lions or two small Mexican cats, the ocelot and the jaguarundi.

Once again, Ron insisted on an early start the following morning. Only now there were ominous gray clouds thick with rain. We donned foul weather gear over wool sweaters and pants to ward off the chill. The thought of capsizing in these cold waters gave me the shivers.

A few more Class I's and II's shoved us out of the canyon's confining walls. Taking their place was Las Vegas de los Ladrones or Outlaw Flats, an expansive, table-smooth grassland. As we paddled against the fresh breeze, it was easy to daydream about people and events here of long ago: when Comanches made life tough for ranchers who dared to intrude; when Mexican bandits made hit-and-run raids into Texas; when mountainmen like Pegleg Smith, Old Bill Williams and Kit Carson led packhorses loaded with beaver pelts through the roughshod Rio Grande valley; and when

Texas Rangers were the only peacemakers in a state larger than many countries.

This reverie was interrupted by the hulking shape of El Capitan, a huge, flat-topped butte thrusting skyward a thousand feet over the monotonous desert plains. In the distance beyond was a hint of the great limestone vaults we would enter in the afternoon.

The miles passed quickly as our paddles worked in unison with the river's four- to five-knot current. After a quick lunch, we shot into the corridor of Big Canyon. The narrow canyon, with its unclimbable walls and lively rapids, was a welcome diversion from the ghost-filled vegas we had left behind.

The next few days were the most exciting, providing us all with hefty doses of adrenaline. At Hot Springs Rapid, a series of holes and chutes created by a giant boulder outwash, one look at the Class III suckholes convinced us to portage. With miles of wild canyon still to come, there was no sense risking an upset or injury.

An unexpected fringe benefit after the portage was a natural riverside hot spring. It didn't take much urging for us to strip off our grimy clothes and ease into this Rio Grande-style hot tub. The worst part of this exquisite experience was leaving the 100-degree water for the 45-degree air above.

Five hours of paddling the next day brought us to more challenging whitewater. Called Burro Bluff Rapid, or Upper Madison Falls, this drop is divided into two sets: an upper half possible to run in open boats and a lower half considered suitable for decked craft and expert paddlers. Since only Louie had the kayak, and the rest of us weren't sure just how "expert" we were, we all paddled through the first rapids while only Louie tackled the rest.

We spent the following two days paddling through changing canyons. The walls got higher and the river grew faster as we flowed closer to Langtry. Except for a few gallons of water that sloshed aboard, we bounced through Horseshoe Falls (also called Lower Madison Rapid) and Panther Creek Rapid with no difficulty.

Below Panther Canyon we crossed a wide fissure that juts into the river from the Texas side. This was San Francisco Canyon, almost as impressive as the Rio Grande gorge itself. An early explorer to these parts described the water-polished tributary as being "marked by queer, eccentric pinnacles projecting above the ragged skyline-spires, fingers, needles, natural bridges and every conceivable form of peaked and curved rocks." Unfortunately, we could spend only a brief time hiking up the never-ending canyon. With a schedule to keep, we returned to the boats and continued downstream.

The last rapid at Sanderson Canyon was a tricky one and we opted for a cheater route along the Mexican side. Beyond Sanderson the high rock continued for another 20 miles until the steep walls gradually lowered and the horizon began to unfold. The federally protected Wild and Scenic Rio Grande had finally come to an end. In its place were overgrazed ranches, barbwire fences and gravel roads. When a Mexican vaquero, or cowboy, dressed like a character out of an old Western movie, rode up to the river and waved to us, we suddenly realized he was the first person we had seen during the past week and a half.

We were sorry to leave the canyons, a lonely, little-traveled land, with discoveries still to be made. We pushed on for the old cowboy town of Langtry, home of Judge Roy Bean—"the Law west of the Pecos"—and his Jersey Lilly Saloon. Here, over an ice-cold beer, we toasted the lower canyons of the Rio Grande.

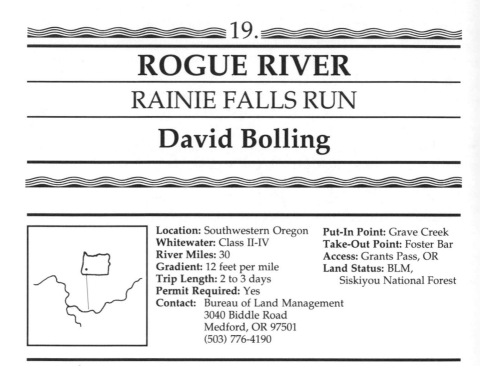

19.

ROGUE RIVER

RAINIE FALLS RUN

David Bolling

Location: Southwestern Oregon
Whitewater: Class II-IV
River Miles: 30
Gradient: 12 feet per mile
Trip Length: 2 to 3 days
Permit Required: Yes
Contact: Bureau of Land Management
3040 Biddle Road
Medford, OR 97501
(503) 776-4190

Put-In Point: Grave Creek
Take-Out Point: Foster Bar
Access: Grants Pass, OR
Land Status: BLM,
Siskiyou National Forest

A dirty gray sky hangs low over the Rogue River, dripping like a wet sponge on the golden-haired German shepherd who stands guarding a mountainous mound of boxes and bags. Enough food, beer and wine is scattered across the boat ramp at Grave Creek to last us a month on the river; there is enough equipment to outfit a major expedition into the wilderness. The three of us plan to be gone about a week.

We have prepared for every appetite and nearly every need. Not trusting the fickle favors of the river or our limited angling skills, we have brought with us one whole salmon, countless steaks, chops and pieces of pre-marinated chicken, fruits, vegetables and gourmet ice cream. We have clothes for every climate, a gas stove, charcoal briquettes and a firewood saw. Our library includes Paul Theroux, Robert Parker, Studs Terkel, Rita Mae Brown, Joseph Wambaugh,

114

Ed Abbey, William Least Heat Moon and Pablo Neruda. On tape, we have music ranging from the Beatles to Bach.

This is going to be a serious retreat from society, an escape from responsibility, deadlines, telephones, red lights, speed limits, neon and noise. Somewhere in the depths of the Rogue River Canyon we are determined to find a warp in space and time. We just hope it will be big enough to accommodate our gear.

The fantasy has grown through a long vacationless summer and into fall; just three of us—a man, a woman and a dog—for eight days alone on the river. We want to heal some wounds, reestablish contact with ourselves, touch the center of being.

So we have come to the Rogue, one of the nation's first official Wild and Scenic rivers, a lush green gash in the coastal mountains of southwestern Oregon, home of beaver, bear, otter, osprey, sturgeon, steelhead and, who knows, maybe the elusive Sasquatch.

But even Bigfoot can't beg or borrow eight days on the Rogue from the end of May to the beginning of September. During that permit season, in fact, a noncommercial boater is lucky to get on the river at all. Fewer than one in nine private applicants succeed. Between Memorial Day and Labor Day the Rogue carries a crush of more than 10,000 people and, while the Forest Service tries to space them along the river's 34-mile wilderness corridor, you're never really alone.

Come fall, the Rogue is a very different river. Its sun-baked surface grows chilly, the sky clouds up, rain falls and moody mists hang over the water. The traffic changes too. Armadas of rafters and fleets of orange inflatable kayaks give way to drift boats and sober-faced fishermen searching for steelhead in the river's riffles and bottomless pools.

Most of these fisherfolk hole up nights in the Rogue's rustic riverside lodges, leaving the beaches to private trips like ours. As the season grows older and colder, virtually any campsite is up for grabs—which is a good thing since we are going to need the better part of a large beach just to unload our supplies.

For us the Rogue is an annual pilgrimage. But we've never been here this late in the year, we've never stretched it to eight days, we've never done it without others to share the cooking and cleaning and riverside palaver. As we climb into our boats, I am inexplicably anxious. With Ellen at the oars of the Miwok, Pablo playing guard dog on top of the ice chest and me in my kayak, we set out into the mid-morning gloom.

We bounce through Grave Creek rapid, and as I paddle through the drizzle toward Rainie Falls I am suddenly seized by a sense of profound isolation. This is clearly a different river from the Rogue we have known. The water isn't warm and inviting now. There is no temptation to slide beneath its jade-green surface to play. Instead, it is cold, mysterious, brooding, the color of molten lead; it seems to be concealing secrets I don't want to know. As I float with it, an ancient fear awakens in some back corner of my mind and takes a terrifying shape. It is an irrational impression and I resist it. But gradually the suspicion grows that somewhere beneath the Rogue's inscrutable surface there is lurking a primordial monster, some slimy green thing with a dragon's tongue and horrible teeth. It has been there all my life, I realize, hiding in a closet of my imagination since childhood. A chill runs through me and I have the feeling we are finally going to meet.

But even subliminal monsters can't compete with the roar from Rainie Falls, which drifts upcanyon, carrying the inevitable, stomach-churning question: to take the plunge or not? Rainie, a genuine waterfall and whitewater legend, carries most of the river over a 15-foot ledge into a chaos of angry water. Even here the Rogue is not unkind. It offers three basic options: a safe but bumpy Class II fish ladder around the right, an anxiety-provoking Class III dory chute entered through a maze of rocks perilously close to the edge, and a heart-stopping Class V drop over the main falls into a maelstrom of hysterical hydraulics and angry foam.

I have run all three routes and know their respective attractions. The fish ladder is safe and sane and even fun, but it lacks the elemental attraction of risk. The dory chute has a nerve-wracking entry with a roller-coaster finish and if you miss the entry you can find yourself plummeting out of control over the worst part of the falls. The big drop itself combines an explosive adrenaline charge of excitement with the terrifying possibility of sudden death. When you run the falls, life is compressed into the very brief but infinitely elastic time frame of about five seconds.

There is no one at Rainie we need to impress and no reason to violate the mood of this trip; we follow the fish ladder downstream.

By the time we clear Rainie and float into the upper reaches of China Gulch it is well past lunchtime, so we pull into a tranquil anchorage at Rum Creek. There we establish what will become the prevailing pace of the trip. We don't move for two days. Instead, we eat, we drink, we read, we sleep. We sit silently on our private beach watching osprey dive-bomb the river as salmon roil the surface and orange newts school at the water's edge.

Slowly the memory of motors and mirrors and Big Macs begins to fade. Slowly we begin to arrive at where we are. We would stay a week on this sleepy spit of sand, but in two days we've gone less than three miles and at this pace we will run out of Cabernet and Haagen-Dazs before the halfway point. We move on.

With rain tickling the water and a sullen sun making random appearances, we bounce through the Rogue's gentle Class III rapids, down Tyee and Wildcat, Russian and Montgomery creeks, the Howard Chutes, Slim Pickens and Plowshare. Except for two major rapids waiting downstream (and the possible presence of that slimy-green monster), the Rogue is worry-free, with enough surfing waves and friendly holes for endless kayak play.

The next day inertia overwhelms us again. Seduced by a rare ration of sunshine, we camp beside Whiskey Creek, which plunges over a waterfall into the Rogue. We loll about on riverside rocks like lazy seals, unable to muster the motivation to break camp. The very thought of reloading the Miwok sends us into spasms of sleep.

Another day passes and we take another step backward into a primordial mindset where cars and clocks don't count, where the heartbeat of a nervous deer is something we can almost feel, where the rhythms of weather and water are all that matter. At times like this I can sense civilization ebbing right out of my pores. I can feel the beard growing on my soul and I know there's something important in this brooding canyon that's printed on the pattern of my genes.

But then another night goes by and the tension of time returns. This odyssey has limits. Somewhere someone is still keeping track.

The morning is moist as we clean our commissary and pack our black bags. The river seems unfriendly. I can't see past the surface of the big pool below our camp and I find myself wondering if the amorphous monster is down there waiting, biding its time for a confrontation I've avoided since I was three. Ellen gives me a chance to find out. A hand-painted plastic plate slips from her hand, bounces down the rocky waterfall into the river and disappears into that deep, dark pool.

We could leave it; we have enough tableware to entertain Lady Di. But it's a favorite plate, and there's the ethic of not dumping debris in the river.

Among my toys I have a mask and fins. I've been wondering when I'll use them and now I know. I stare at the moody surface a long time, remembering monsters under my childhood bed, fighting the irrational fear that something unknown and overwhelming lurks below. I struggle to put a face on this fear, to impose some reason on the unreasonable belief that there could be something real and menacing beneath the surface of the Rogue. I dive.

The falls from Whiskey Creek aerate the water and I see nothing but bubbles and a cluster of curious minnows the first 10 feet down. I dive deeper into the startlingly deep pool and then, far below on the bottom, I see the familiar white plate with the crude painted picture of me hanging inverted in a kayak.

I grab the plate, look around me, and find the green surface far above with shafts of feeble sunlight filtering down. Suddenly I realize I'm inside the Rogue, enveloped in its body, a body that has the shape of a long, liquid, sinuous serpent. I feel strangely safe. Have I swum into the belly of the beast? Have I confronted the demon? I'm not sure. It occurs to me that the monster in the closet of my mind may not live in the river; it may be the river.

With a light rain falling, we move downstream, pursued by another kind of demon. Something we ate has attacked us. Ellen is feverish and pulls the oars painfully. My joints ache, my head feels hot. It starts to rain again. We are miserable.

The fever in our bodies and the gloom in the sky conspire to make Horseshoe Bend seem sullen and ominous. In the erratic eddies boiling past the apex of the oxbow, the Rogue seems to be rearranging itself into some tortured new configuration. Maybe here the river simply carries a watery memory of the twisted life of Dutch Henry, a recluse who lived in a nearby meadow and is suspected of murdering a few miners.

By early afternoon we are both feverish, exhausted and barely able to unload the boat at Quail Creek and set up camp. It is a cold and rainy night and all we can stomach from our gourmet larder is miso soup. We sprawl into the tent, Pablo's wet, smelly body pressed in beside us. We spend the next day recovering, collecting firewood, reading and watching a family of frolicking otters slide in and out of the water like oil. We eat dinner in the rain, feeding a giant campfire to keep warm.

By now we have covered 13 miles in six days. We aren't halfway down the river and we have two days left. It is time to move. In the morning we load the Miwok with painful speed and are on the water by noon.

We drift peacefully past Battle Bar where more than 500 U.S. Cavalry troops attacked a contingent of 200 Rogue Indians, mostly women and children, during the bitter Indian wars of the 1850s. The Rogues were named by French trappers but they identified themselves as people of the Takelma and Tutuni tongues. White miners invaded the canyon in 1851 on the heels of the California gold rush and tried to push the Indians out. The result was a two-year series of "encounters" the Indians inevitably lost. They were banished to reservations where half of them immediately died, and now only their ghostly spirits hang in the river mist.

Zane Grey's cabin at Winkle Bar is surrounded by a congregation of reverent anglers as we pass. They look like worshippers at a shrine. Grey was a formidable fisherman and wrote many of his frontier novels here, weaving in tales he heard on the Rogue.

Finally we near the narrow mouth of Mule Creek Canyon, a place unlike any other on any river. It is a long, deep, rock-lined chasm so tight you can almost touch both sides with extended fingertips. A raft spun sideways by the current can wedge between the walls until a surging eddy sucks down a tube and flips the boat.

The rain-swollen river is higher than I've ever seen it as Ellen enters the canyon, Pablo standing upright in canine concern as the raft is sucked into the rocky tunnel. I follow, bracing carefully, paddling tentatively. Too tentatively.

For years I have belittled accounts of the Coffeepot, a surging explosion of turbulence midway through the canyon, which guidebooks claim can boil you worse than campfire coffee. I have never before encountered its fury, but suddenly I am in the middle of it, a mad convergence of upwelling water trying to go in every direction at once. There is no coherent current.

The Coffeepot forces me into the canyon wall, then slams me against a rock outcrop. I am upside down, looking into that ominous darkness before I know what has hit me.

Clearly I have not yet made peace with the monster. I feel a stab of claustrophobic fear as dark images flash through my mind. The persistent impression of some bestial presence beneath me conspires with the weird water to defeat my first attempt to roll. I set up and do it again and as my head breaks the surface and the water clears from my eyes, I look around for the Miwok. It is gone.

I move forward with the current, suddenly bewildered. I haven't been upside down that long. Am I trapped in my own nightmare?

Has Mule Creek Canyon swallowed the Miwok whole? Are Ellen and Pablo caught in the jaws of the jabberwocky? I paddle madly, the current throwing me ahead. No sign of the raft.

Then my kayak encounters more turbulence, slows, spins halfway around and the silly truth hits me. My roll has turned me upstream and the Coffeepot's crazy, contrary currents have carried me in the wrong direction. Over my shoulder I can see the Miwok moving sedately downriver, upright and under control.

The last real challenge on the Rogue is Blossom Bar, a beautifully congested slalom course of water-sculpted house-sized rocks, which, until 1930, was so choked with stone that there was no passage through it. But then the legendary riverman Glen Wooldridge blew the worst rocks out of the river, creating a zig-zag channel.

Wooldridge's demolition strategy was simple: he filled a gunnysack with dynamite and stone, worked his skiff up behind the offending boulder, lit the fuse, dumped the bag and then rowed like crazy downstream.

We slip through Blossom in the late afternoon sun, whooping as we clear the last rock, and then stop at the bottom to inspect the splintered ruins of a wooden drift boat that hasn't been so lucky.

It is still light when we reach a broad, empty beach below Tate Creek for our final camp. We have covered 15 miles since noon, more than the previous six days combined. We are back on schedule, once more obeying the clock.

As darkness falls and mist rises in the Douglas fir, a full moon creeps over the eastern horizon and traces a glowing trail along the ridge behind us. We eat our dinner, drink the last of our vintage wine, stack the wood we've gathered into an enormous pyre and watch the flames drive back the night.

The week has been cold and wet and sometimes dreary, nothing like the sunny summer frolics we are familiar with. We have seen the dark side of the Rogue, and its gloomy surface has mirrored back to me frightening images of fears I thought were dead. But sitting in the fading firelight, with Pablo spread out in the sand like a hairy gargoyle and the river snaking peacefully out of sight, I suddenly realize the truth about this trip. I have met the river for the first time on its own terms, not on mine. It has given me a glimpse of much I yet need to learn. Ellen and I agree that the winter Rogue is a less comfortable, more complex and compelling river. And we agree we would do it again in a minute.

20

THE SALMON RIVER— CALIFORNIA

MAIN RUN

Brian Clark

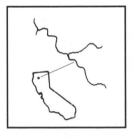

Location: Northwestern California
Whitewater: Class IV-V
River Miles: 14
Gradient: 45 feet per mile
Trip Length: 2 days
Permit Required: No
Contact: Klamath National Forest
1312 Fairlane Road
Yreka, CA 96097
(916) 842-6131

Put-In Point: Nordheimer
Creek Campground
Take-Out Point: Oak
Bottom Campground
Access: Somes Bar, CA
Forks of the Salmon, CA
Land Status: Klamath
National Forest, private

Some call it the Slammin' Salmon, some the Cal Salmon, still others just the plain old Salmon River. Those who've run it a time or two or three—it can be addictive—hang the first moniker on this wild, rapid-strewn river. The second is used by outfitters who want to make sure their clients don't think they're signing up for the more well-known and bigger—but less exciting—Salmon River in Idaho. The last is what locals call it and it's obvious they're talking about their very own stream, one that charges down a gnarled canyon and belongs to a small club of some of the most exciting rivers in the Golden State.

George Wendt, a respected river runner out of Angles Camp, ranks the Cal Salmon up there with the likes of the Tuolumne River,

121

which tumbles down from peaks in Yosemite National Park on its way to the San Joaquin Valley. "If you're only going to do a half a dozen rivers in your lifetime," Wendt has said, "the Cal Salmon has got to be one of them."

Appropriately, something as special as the Cal Salmon can only be run in limited doses. Because it is a wild, dam-free river, the flow is limited to runoff from winter rains—when boating requires a thick wetsuit or drysuit—or else in early summer when snows from in and around the Salmon-Trinity Alps Primitive Area are melting. Its headwaters arise from Sawtooth Peak, the Coast Range's sole glacier. Come late June, the flows of the Slammin' Salmon will have slowed, and boaters who delayed will have to wait until another season rolls around.

It is not without reason that one of the most well-respected kayak schools in the country is found within a stone's throw of the banks of the Cal Salmon. Or that Gayle Wilson, an Oregon video producer, chooses to hang out above rapids like Bloomer Falls, Cascade or Freight Train, and shoot what she calls "crash and burn" footage. So it goes with Class V rivers.

The activity at Bloomer used to be a lot spookier. So much so that many people—wisely—carried their boats around the rapid. It had some of the more powerful hydraulics—especially at higher water—this writer has ever seen. Bloomer Falls did not exist before the huge flood of 1964, which left large trees perched on canyon outcroppings 75 feet above river level. It caused a rock slide at Bloomer, which formed a natural dam and backed the river up. Shortly after the flood, state officials blew up the slide to create the falls.

In 1982, an emergency room doctor and veteran kayaker attempted to run Bloomer Falls at high water and was caught in the hole at the base of the Falls. He was dashed against the rocks, knocked unconscious and drowned. It was that death, most boaters believe, that spelled the end for the old Bloomer Falls. When 1983 rolled around, the California Department of Fish and Game bombed the rapid once again. When they were done, Bloomer Falls was no longer a Class V drop. It is now a Class III or Class III+ and while it is still exciting and offers a good healthy splash, its hydraulics are no longer potentially fatal. Some say, however, that each season since the Fish and Game boys had their way—ostensibly to make it less difficult for salmon to move up the river—Bloomer Falls has been getting a little hairier.

It wasn't to test the river gods that my group of rafters and kayakers was on the Cal Salmon in early June. Armando Duron, a lawyer from Los Angeles who has made challenging river adventures his personal rite of passage, put it this way: "I'm out here for the rapids and the rocks and the canyons. I want to enjoy the river and feel the rush of adrenaline and the surge of excitement. But I really don't have to feel that I've cheated death. I'll leave that to you crazy kayakers."

Led by veteran guide and outdoor photographer Curt Smith, Duron's boat had pushed off from Nordheimer Creek Campground earlier in the morning after a thorough run-down on rafting safety procedures—nothing to scoff at on a river like the Cal Salmon. Less than a mile downstream, Duron's boat was at the lip of Bloomer Falls, tipping down and then crunching into the reversal below. He and his compadres hooted with glee as the raft bucked free and lurched downstream, missing the granite wall on the left by the smallest of margins.

Miners—who followed explorers and Hudson Bay Company trappers into the area—also hooted when they poured into this isolated backcountry during the gold rush of 1850 to 1851. At least some of them did. Most of the miners who came from Hawaii, China, Brazil and even as far away as Africa, only got callouses to show for their hard work.

The Native Americans—Yurok and Karok Indians—who lived along the Salmon, found it a good place to live that was full of deer, elk, beaver and bear. They fared even worse than the immigrant workers. Battles over the land led to killing. Those who survived were marched off to die on the reservations.

On the rocks above Bloomer Falls, video cameras whirred as four boats rocked and rolled through the rapid. My group of three kayakers found a few waves to play on in the stretch below Bloomer. I watched a red-tailed hawk soar in the sky as my friends Bill Bridger and Moth Lorenzen did a dual surf on a wave. Then we peeled out from the eddy into the main current and caught the rafts just in time to see the last boat enter the Maze, a lengthy slalom run through a batch of jumbled boulders, also a gift from the flood of 1964.

Another mile downstream we were in the Salmon River Gorge. I looked up at the canyon walls, just like I'd done a half a dozen times before, and shook my head at the giant trees tossed high on the ledges like so many match sticks. What an incredible amount of water must have come rushing down that twisting gorge. More than 100,000 cubic feet per second. Those logs must have had one hell of a ride, I thought, as we bounced along on a river that was plenty challenging at only a tiny fraction of the flood level.

The video cameras were there again as we entered Cascade, a drop that my friend Bill Bridger knows all too well. The year before, he'd made the top two-thirds of the drop with no problems but the last section was tough on his face. He flipped over and kissed a rock, a blow that broke his glasses and pushed the frame into the flesh around his right eye. Fortunately the eyeball itself was not damaged but the gash took 21 stitches to close.

This time, though, Bill made a flawless run, zipping down the left-hand chute under the watchful eyes of the rafters who lined the wall. Moth's kayak entered on the right, hitting a rock broadside that almost tipped him over. But he dug his paddle into the current and pulled himself off before he dropped into the main rapid. I chose a left slot, nearly repeated his move on another rock, and bounced down through the rest of the run, thanking my lucky stars that I hadn't flipped. After the kayaks, each one of the rafts finessed its way through the boulders and crashed down into the eddy below.

There were more difficult rapids, more waves and a few holes and reversals. Still, the best was yet to come. A little less than six miles into our run we rounded a bend and came to a rapid known as Grants Bluff or Freight Train. Some guides call it Train Wreck for the damage it can do to rafts. It is not a drop you want to swim. Nasty reversals and big rocks and what seem to be river-wide holes can cause even the best boaters to wish they were back at Otter Bar Lodge soaking in the hot tub, drinking a glass of fine wine and having some smooth, aged cheese on a whole wheat cracker.

But we weren't at Otter Bar. And we were not in camp yet. We were at the top of Freight Train. I fought down the lump in my throat and then paddled onto the small, crystal-blue tongue that leads between two sharp rocks. I plopped into a hole, squirted out and caught the big eddy on the right. Moth and Bill came next and I watched as Moth paddled to the left edge of the river, punched into a white haystack and disappeared. I looked at Bill, said "See you at the bottom," and followed Moth's trail.

I figured I'd scoot the haystack to the left, but the river had other ideas. There was a lot more current coming off the wall than I'd anticipated and before I could say "Mercy," I was throwing a big brace downstream and bouncing on the white maelstrom at the top of the big rock. It held me for a second, then released me over the rock and I floated downstream. For some reason the monstrous reversal I'd expected wasn't there. The hole turned out to be a marshmallow.

As Bill came slicing through, I turned to Moth and said, "Piece of cake, eh?"

"Yeah, right, but you wouldn't have known it from the look on your face coming through that last drop," he said, laughing.

As the three of us bobbed in the eddy below, the rafts came careened through Freight Train, seemingly out of control. Yet each time it looked as if they would flip, the boatman would crank on a long oar or call out a command to his crew and the boat would drive forward, keeping itself upright.

That night, as we sat around the campfire, we told stories of other rivers in Peru, Chile, Southern Mexico and Africa, rivers with names like the Apurimac, Jatate, Bio Bio and Zambezi. They were classics of river lore. But they were far away and we were here on a classic in its own right. It didn't require much appreciation of whitewater to see why groups like Friends of the River had lobbied so hard and so long to get the Cal Salmon added to the National Wild and Scenic Rivers System.

Morning and breakfast came and went. We changed into our gear and put back on the river. It was already warm and the splash of the Cal Salmon's chilly water felt good. More Class III and Class IV rapids followed, including Marble. Below, we relaxed in our boats and drifted passed Wooley Creek, a premier trout stream not too far from where President Herbert Hoover once owned a fishing cabin. Then we were into a stretch of mild rapids before our take-out at the Oak Bottom Campground. As we loaded up our kayaks and headed east along the Klamath, not too far from its confluence with the Salmon, dark clouds and raindrops began to fall.

"This keeps up, the Salmon may rise," said Moth, hinting at turning around for another go. But the drops trailed off and responsibility called. Bill stepped on the gas again. "Next year," said Moth. "But when we come back we'll take on the North and South forks too."

21

THE SALMON RIVER— IDAHO

MIDDLE FORK

Jeff Rennicke

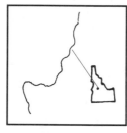

Location: Northern Idaho	**Put-In Point:** Dagger Falls
Whitewater: Class III-IV	**Take-Out Point:** Cache Bar
River Miles: 100	**Access:** Challis, ID
Gradient: 29 Feet per mile	Stanley, ID
Trip Length: 5 to 6 days	**Land Status:** National Forest,
Permit Required: Yes	private
Contact: United States Forest Service	
Challis National Forest	
Challis, ID 83226	
(208) 879-4321	

There wasn't much left to say. I'd already heard all the stories. Anyway, silence in the face of a legend only seems appropriate. Some things—good beer, old hunting knives, certain baseball teams—can inspire an almost unreasonable loyalty. Rivers, too, can be like that. The Middle Fork of the Salmon is such a river. As we drive the rutted dirt road lined with black, shadowy pine trees that leads to the put-in, I watch the face of the driver, Tom Beck, lit by the green glow of the dashboard and think about what he'd said of the Middle Fork.

"It's the only river," Beck had said, sitting around the fire on another river trip, "that I could run, take out and turn right around and paddle down again and again forever." High praise from some-one who has run almost everything the western maps call a "river."

Butch Welch, whom we'd meet downstream, was at the camp-fire on that other river too. As a game warden for the Idaho Fish and Game Department, Butch's job was to run the Middle Fork all summer checking for fishing licenses and game violations. That trip had been was his first away from what had become "his river" over the years. As much as he had enjoyed that other river, one of my favorites, you could tell something was missing. Although he had never said as much, it was in his eyes. It just plain, flat-out, by God was not the Middle Fork of the Salmon.

There is only one Middle Fork and somewhere up ahead, at the end of this road, I'd have my first chance to see the river that holds such a strong spell over river rats like these two.

By the high beams of the headlights, it doesn't look like much— shallow and spiked with rocks. But with the engine shut off, the sound of it carries in the dark, a sound like a clear breeze that has come a long way to play in the wind chimes. Come first light, it would be time for all the stories to stop and for our trip down the legend to begin.

Despite the fact that the river maps list Dagger Falls put-in as mile 0, the river actually starts a few miles upstream where Bear Valley meets Marsh Creek. But it's all semantics. The Middle Fork is one of the only chances paddlers have in the lower 48 states to run the full length of a wild river from its headwaters to its mouth. That's a part of what makes the Middle Fork so special in many river runners' hearts. It is a complete river and paddling it from top to bottom is like hearing a whole song instead of just a few chopped-up notes.

The chorus of the song is in the more than 35 rated rapids that rumble in its course—15 of which are rated Class III or higher. They begin early. It's almost continuous whitewater during the first five miles of the river below the 60-foot-long wooden ramp that is used to slide rafts to the water.

Pushing a raft into the current of the Middle Fork is a little like jumping out a window. There is no time to recheck the knots in the rigging. As the third boat out, I watch the others plunge around the corner just downstream and then proceed to smash into the rock that they all missed and snap an oar. Not a good start and the raft plays pinball against the rocks until I can slap a spare in the oarlock.

The Middle Fork is a nervous river, shallow and technical, with a pattern that is hard to read. That is one of the challenges and one of the beauties. Within a bend or two, I get the feel of it—through the unnamed Class II rapids, the Class III rock garden called Sulphur Slide and, like a crescendo, Velvet Falls, a Class IV drop at mile 5.4, which signals a lull in the whitewater storm.

With the roar of Velvet Falls fading behind, there is time to drift and look at the river. The Middle Fork is a mountain river, clear, cold and tucked between shores fringed with ponderosa and lodgepole pine whose branches reflect in the water and make the river flow the color of jade. Its course cuts through parts of four national forests and through the 2.2-million-acre River-of-No-Return Wilderness area. It is a wild river and that wildness was recognized in 1968 when the Middle Fork became one of the eight original rivers protected by the passage of the National Wild and Scenic Rivers Act.

Between the rapids, the water goes still in deep, dark pools where redsides, the local name for cutthroat trout that are thick as your forearm, circle and feed. As we drift quietly, I hear a soft whipping noise. In the boat ahead someone has broken out the fly rod. Against the light of early evening, the line looks like a strand of sunshine arcing across the water.

The water is flowing high for this late in July—3.2 feet on the gauge—but it is low on a river that can run 5 feet, 6 feet, 6.5 feet on the gauge, levels that are listed respectively by the Forest Service as "normal hazard," "extreme" and "suicidal." The low water exposes a long gravel bench at the landing to Sheepeater Camp, meaning a long pull to shore to tie up the boats. But the water in the river is not what matters at this camp. It is another kind of water, not in the river, not in the sidecreeks. It is as clear and beautiful as the water there, but it is something more: hot.

Dozens of natural hot springs line the river's corridor, and the pool at Sheepeater Camp is one of the most popular. We land the boats, set up our tents beneath the pines, grab a bottle of river-chilled wine and walk up the small bench behind camp to the springs.

Once, the pool was housed in a log cabin built by miners who came here to soothe their knotted muscles. Long before that, the Indians of the area, called the Sheepeaters for the mountain sheep they hunted in the canyon, considered the waters of the hot springs sacred and filled with medicine. Some things have changed along the river but one thing has not. The hard-barked miners, the Indians, even the Tappen boys who once homesteaded here would recognize the feeling of lowering a tired body into the warm waters. We toast to their memories and then sit back to watch the stars slowly knit the night sky above us.

Even with all the stories I've heard, there is one more that I'd like to know the end of. It starts with a great old photograph in one of the guidebooks of a group of rafters rounding the bend at Pistol Creek Rapid, an S-turn Class IV run in a tight canyon, only to find the mouth of the rapid clogged with huge snags spanning the entire channel. It is a classic display of the power in a wild river and a classic dilemma for boaters. The caption offers no clue. In the old photo the rafts forever hang in the balance and I am still waiting, as if for the other shoe to drop, to hear the rest of the story.

We have no such trouble in Pistol Creek. We sit a long time along the cliffs below the rapid, watching the blue-green water go white in the canyon and then settle dark beyond. Where the water settles after the rapid, we meet up with Butch who leads us downstream.

Butch is a stout barrel of a man with a full growth of beard thicker than a mule's hide and eyes that wear the constant squint of one used to staring down poachers and horizons. Around the campfire telling stories, he looks like he would fit in just fine with the string of characters in the Middle Fork's history, men like Fred Paulson who could hold up a loaded haywagon while a wooden wheel was repaired; Dutch Charlie Rockland who homesteaded at Little Loon Creek, did his own dental work on himself and even set his own broken leg; or the hermit Earl Parrott who built his own version of paradise along the river and left notes on his cabins claiming "the cork came out of that bottle of Poison" to scare off possible looters. A few weather-beaten cabins along the river, the monument of antlers marking the grave of Whitey Cox, the faint outlines of pictographs on rock walls, only those few things remain of these lives, but in the dim light around the campfire, they seem to throw off the years and flow on like the river.

At Cougar Ranch, under a bright sun, Butch leads us to a bench just above the river. There in the weeds is a simple circle of stones, the ring that once held down the corners of a skin tent of the Sheepeaters. It is only a few rocks, but even under the warm sun it is not hard to imagine the family curled beneath their hide blankets 200 autumns ago as a hard wind rattled in the poles above them. We stand for a moment, thinking, and then hike back down to the rafts.

Much of the upper river winds through rolling, timbered hills with long horizons. But the shadows slowly grow darker on the water and the walls begin to rise more steeply. Below Wilson Creek the river begins its descent into the edge of the jagged Bighorn Crags and starts to cut what is called the Impassable Canyon. Details of the first trip down the Middle Fork and through the Impassable Canyon are sketchy with age and the telling, but it is believed that Captain Harry Guleke made the maiden voyage early in the 1900s reportedly "sometimes . . . on the raft and sometimes . . . under it."

Someone is reading that quote out of the guidebook at this our last camp, near Cliffside Rapid. The weather has closed in and clouds gather in the canyon downstream, making it look even more impassable. We've already come through some bigwater—Redside, Porcupine and Weber rapids just upstream. But below us in the 15 or so miles to the confluence lie seven rapids rated Class III or above, with names like Devil's Tooth, Jump-Off, Hancock and, the biggest water on the river, Rubber Rapid. The rolling of thunder all night in the canyon sounds like the roar of rapids downstream.

By morning the sun is out, the clouds are gone and the canyon looks much more inviting. Butch and Beck team up to cook a huge trail breakfast. Since this is the last day on the river, everything goes, even a cold meatball from last night's spaghetti.

On the water the rapids come fast, and like the first few miles of the trip, they go by in a blur. The sun is hard and edgeless, making the canyon walls seem almost white, but there is not much time to look around. It is almost constant whitewater action. I keep my raft in sight of Butch and Beck who know the river, and we run most of the rapids without scouting. In House Rock, I lose sight of them around the huge boulders and nearly slip into a wrong, dead-end channel before noticing it at the last moment, and spin the boat to the right side of the rock.

This is one of the most interesting, exciting sections of river I've ever run, and like all good things—good beer and baseball games included—it goes by too fast. I see Butch float out into a grayer, wider river and know we are at the confluence with the Main Salmon. There are another four miles down the Main Salmon before the take-out, but to me the trip ends where the clear water of the Middle Fork goes dark with the big river.

Quickly, the strong current of the big river pulls us downstream and the canyon of the Middle Fork closes from our view. We float close together for a time, talking a little. Almost as soon as we are out of sight of the river, the Middle Fork stories start again. They are all true, or at least close enough for river stories. The Middle Fork, like all good wild rivers, is a river of stories, a place where the mind can rush back through each of the rapids or curl slowly like an eddy against a cliff wall where the shadows go deep and the cutthroat swim.

Butch is quiet, listening to the stories this time, as if gauging our reaction as he lets his boat drift close to ours.

"That's quite a river you've got there, Butch," I say finally, as the take-out swings into view.

"Yup," he says, knowing full well that at the next campfire, whatever river it may be on, I'll be the one telling stories, and the legend of the Middle Fork will grow with each telling. "Yup, that it is."

22.

THE SALMON RIVER— IDAHO

WILD RIVER SEGMENT

Verne Huser

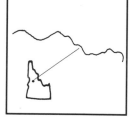

Location: Central Idaho
Whitewater: Class II-IV
River Miles: 79
Gradient: 12 feet per mile
Trip Length: 5 to 7 days
Permit Required: Yes
Contact: North Fork District Ranger
Salmon National Forest
P.O. Box 780, North Fork, ID 83466
(208) 865-2383

Put-In Point: Corn Creek
Take-Out Point: Chittam Boat Ramp
Access: Salmon, ID
Riggins, ID
Land Status: Frank Church
River-of-No-Return Wilderness

Nothing so epitomizes Idaho as the Salmon River, one of the longest undammed rivers in the West. Known as the River-of-No-Return, the entire Salmon system lies within the Gem State. While its tributaries have been adversely affected by the mining, logging and agricultural practices that create the economy of the state, there is not a major dam in the entire drainage.

Before European civilization reached the Salmon River, the local Indians had named the river for the chinook salmon that spawned in its pristine waters. In 1805 the Salmon River forced the Lewis and Clark Expedition to find an overland route to the Pacific. Much of Idaho's history centers on the Salmon River: the gold rush, the Indian wars, the homesteaders.

Today the river is part of the National Wild and Scenic Rivers System: a 79-mile segment of the Salmon has been designated Wild; a 46-mile segment, Recreational.

I first floated the Salmon the summer of 1970, running the entire wild segment on a private trip with writers Rod Nash and Bob Collins. During the next dozen years I came to know the Salmon River well as I guided trips on the River-of-No-Return and returned often to run private trips. That first trip on the Salmon carried an interesting crew: two vice-chancellors, two professors and four students from the University of California, Santa Barbara. That was the summer immediately following the burning of the Bank of America branch just off the UCSB campus to protest the Vietnam War. There were some lively discussions around the campfire every evening.

The river was lively too, a mid-summer clear green but higher than most years. Six people died on the Middle Fork and the Main Salmon that spring and summer, a high-water year. Two were killed on the Middle Fork only a month earlier, which Tom Brokaw wrote about in his memorable article, "That River Swallows People. Some It Gives Up. Some It Don't."

Rod and Bob had just negotiated the Middle Fork when I joined them at Cache Bar, bringing in supplies—ice, beer, fresh meat and vegetables—for five more days on the river. We had no problems until we hit Middle Split Rock Rapid the next day.

I was in Rod's boat a hundred yards ahead of Bob's. As we drifted through a little rapid, we noticed a nasty rock in the midst of a wave that created a serious hole. We tried to signal Bob, but no one in his boat was looking. His boat hit the hole, wallowed about for a moment, then came through upright. Everyone was still in the boat, but all of them were swimming. They had taken on a boat-load of river—and lost two hard-hat helmets that the vice chancellors were wearing, university issue for riot control. We retrieved one of them miles downstream later that day.

Middle Split Rock came back to haunt me years later after I'd run the river a dozen times. In 1978, leading a private trip with the late writer and photographer David Sumner, I failed to forewarn him about the potential problem. He flipped. My first knowledge of it was when someone in my boat said, "Dave's over."

I looked back to see the bottom of the raft and several heads bobbing down the river. "Count heads!" I yelled and began rowing toward the disabled craft. Everyone was on the surface, four of them clinging to the Miwok II raft and a fifth swimming toward shore in an eddy. I threw the safety line. Dave caught it, but it was jerked from his grasp as the rope went taut from the full force of the current that was dragging his boat downstream and my boat out of the eddy.

I pulled it in, filled the bag with river and threw again. This time Les caught it and tied it to the raft.

We streaked through Lower Split Rock like a pair of binary stars revolving around each other in a meteorite shower. I kept trying to row into an eddy, only to have Dave's raft, its oars deep in the water catching current, serve as a sea anchor that pulled me back into the current time after time. We raced downstream, I in frustration and near exhaustion, Dave and his crew in the river, getting colder by the minute.

Finally I saw Dave approaching my boat, pulling himself hand-over-hand along the taut safety line. "I'm ready to get out of the water now," he said, and we pulled him aboard. The others followed, one by one, as they too used the taut line to approach my raft—all but my 10-year-old nephew Maki. He had to stay with the overturned raft through still another rapid before we could retrieve him.

Finally we were able to stop the binary action, tie up to shore and get some dry clothes out of the drypacks. We treated for mild hypothermia and rested in the sun as we assessed the situation.

What had happened to the swimmer? Someone had seen her reach shore. Before we could organize a search party to hike back upstream, she was delivered by another river party that had picked her up. She was already dry and feeling great, ready to help with the righting of the raft, which we accomplished in short order. We headed downstream once more, but our confidence was shaken. And Big Mallard, a Class IV rapid, considered by many to be one of the 10 toughest rapids in the West, lay in wait a few miles downstream.

We decided to camp.

From our campsite at Camp Creek, we had ample time to scout Big Mallard and to discuss the day's adventure. We could hear the roar of the rapid we'd be running in the morning. We sat for more than an hour after dinner, parked on the rocks overlooking Big Mallard from the right bank, then gathered around the campfire to process the flip. What had gone wrong? How did it happen? What might we have done to prevent it or avoid it? What might we have done better? Quicker? We were somewhat apprehensive. A capsize takes the wind out of one's sails, saps the confidence, initiates the doubts.

We talked it to death around the fire and, as it died, I began to tell about other Big Mallard runs . . . like the first one. Rod, Bob and I had stopped to scout it, decided on a right-hand run and launched. Rod was leading once more, and I was still in his boat—for a moment. We knew where we wanted to run but couldn't get there. We went into a gigantic hole below the rock left of center, flipping like a coin.

I was the only one thrown free of the boat. The others all stayed with the craft and I reached shore before they did. I was scared, wet and cold, but we soon warmed in the hot summer sun and dried out as we worked to right the boat. It was no small feat; it took all the strength of 10 strong men to pull the ancient military surplus craft right side up.

Another time I ran Big Mallard at 33,000 cubic feet per second. There was no hole on the left; the entire rapid was washed out and there were five or six standing waves on the right— 12, 14, 16 feet high. Even in a 27-foot pontoon boat at 33,000 cubic feet per second, this rapid gives you the thrill of your life.

I recalled the stories of other Big Mallard mishaps: the 1936 Hatch-Swain trip when three out of four boats flipped in the legendary rapid as related in Cort Conley's *River of No Return*. It was also a nemesis for Captain Harry Guleke, who ran wooden scows down the Salmon for more than 40 years beginning before the turn of the century. Even the Craighead brothers had trouble here during their 1968 National Geographic filming expedition.

Before we ran Big Mallard the next morning, another party, up early and on the river before us, ran it and gave us the advantage of watching them. They ran the slot on the left, as I had learned long ago was the way to run it. I'd never scouted the rapid from the right before, but we could see clearly that at this water level it was the only way to go. Finally we launched and made as fine a run as I can remember. All our confidence came back as we finessed Big Mallard.

The Salmon River isn't all rapids by any means. In fact, it is a pretty mellow river at the normal mid-summer water levels between 6,000 and 16,000 cubic feet per second. There are no terrifying rapids, lots of sandy beaches—a benefit of no dams upstream—and great swimming in clear, cool water. The fishing can be good when you run into a school of dolly varden, as we did one day at the mouth of California Creek. The three kids on our family-reunion trip caught their limit before their parents could get their gear operational.

I caught one of the finest rainbow trout of my life during a layover day at Groundhog Bar. Fishing in the tributary streams can be excellent. Salmon and steelhead still run in the river, but since Idaho is at the end of the line for adromous fish, fishing seasons have been limited by the need to allow fish to pass for spawning.

Historically the Salmon offers early homesteads, old mines, ancient pictographs and more modern inscriptions. At Barth Hot Springs, Johnny McKay left his name carved into the rock with the dates 1872, 1905 and 1911. Native Americans are known to have lived along the Salmon for at least 8,500 years.

On my first Salmon River trip in the summer of 1970, homesteader Frank Lantz was still alive. I have since visited his old place frequently, sampling the strawberries (now pretty well overgrown with poison ivy) and the wild fruit in his orchard. At Rhett Creek we used to have rhubarb cobbler almost every trip from a pioneer plant gone wild over the decades.

During my September 1977 trip, the apples were ripe all up and down the Salmon. The bears had found them and had made a shambles of the orchards, breaking down branches to get at the fruit and leaving their droppings everywhere. Jim Campbell, who owned Shepp Ranch for years, told me he'd once seen 13 bears in his orchard on a moonlit night in early autumn.

On that same trip, we spent three hours at Buckskin Bill's place. Buckskin's gone now—died the spring of 1980 at age 74—but his place is still there, with his grave nearby. The inscription on his tombstone reads:

Sylvan A. Hart
"Buckskin Bill"
May 10, 1906 April 29, 1980
The Last of the Mountain Men
Erected by his Friends,
the Ed-da-how Long Rifles, June, 1980

Buckskin moved to the Salmon River country at the height of the Great Depression and lived there "off the fat of the land" for almost a half a century. He was a part of the Salmon River. Everyone who ran the Salmon in those days stopped to visit him for a tour of his stockade, garden and fort. He was a showman, to be sure, and he entertained his visitors with wild garb and relics of the wilderness like the mountain lion embryos he kept in a pickle jar.

He was also a craftsman. He made his own knives, rifles, pots and pans; everything he made, while utilitarian, was also a work of art. He was well read and gregarious, and he lived alone at the mouth of Five Mile Creek in the heart of the wilderness. The Salmon River isn't the same without him.

There is also the Jim Moore place, a historic site where the original cabins still stand. It is, as Cort Conley says in *River of No Return*, "an impressive tribute" to the skill of the craftsman who built them near the turn of the century.

And finally, there is Shepp Ranch at the mouth of Crooked Creek where I once spent a week between Christmas and New Year's Day visiting Jim and Anita Douglas Campbell. The main cabin was built in 1910. It now serves as the kitchen, where, in an ancient wood-burning stove, they cooked a turkey and pumpkin pies. Seeing the Salmon River country during winter was a special thrill. On the way in, we'd seen a cougar stalking a bull elk. Every evening we saw dozens of elk on the ridge above the ranch.

Salmon River history comes alive at Shepp Ranch, where Jim established several museums commemorating the various occupations practiced in the canyon: mining, ranching, timber cutting. Several graves add to the sense of history of the ranch. The orchard and garden supply food as they did decades ago when the first settlers planted them.

The Salmon offers the best family river trip I can imagine, with insights into archaeology and history, good camping and swimming beaches, excellent fishing and exciting—but not terrifying—whitewater rapids. There is abundant wildlife, and the wildflowers are glorious. By mid-August the autumn color begins in the ground cover. In September, with hunting season and steelhead time on the river, the Salmon River country is at its best. Winters are long but often remarkably mild. The river usually, but not always, freezes up. Mid-spring (April, early May) is a good time to run the river if you can beat the runoff that brings flood stages by late May or early June.

The Salmon offers many fond memories to this river runner: skipping rocks on the shingle beach across from the mouth of Crooked Creek; the beach in front of the Polly Bemis place; seeing otter in the river from a campsite on the beach by the big eddy just above Lantz Bar; watching bighorn sheep grazing like domestic livestock on a river bench, soaking in the hot tub fed by natural springs a mile above Barth Hot Springs; the visits with Buckskin Bill. The Salmon River has much to offer. Each individual finds his or her own peace with the Salmon. It is a renewing place to spend a day or a week or as long as you like. A lot of people return to the River-of-No-Return for it's a favorite spot with those who want to get away to a real wilderness experience.

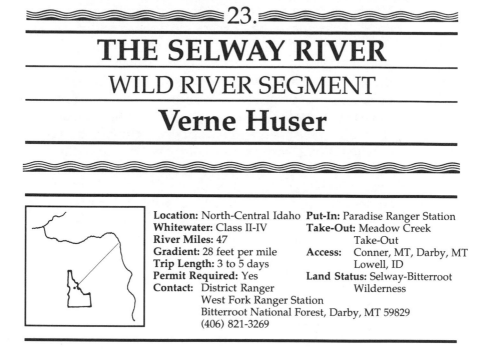

23.

THE SELWAY RIVER

WILD RIVER SEGMENT

Verne Huser

Location: North-Central Idaho
Whitewater: Class II-IV
River Miles: 47
Gradient: 28 feet per mile
Trip Length: 3 to 5 days
Permit Required: Yes
Contact: District Ranger
West Fork Ranger Station
Bitterroot National Forest, Darby, MT 59829
(406) 821-3269

Put-In: Paradise Ranger Station
Take-Out: Meadow Creek
Take-Out
Access: Conner, MT, Darby, MT
Lowell, ID
Land Status: Selway-Bitterroot
Wilderness

All my river-running life, it seems, I have been applying for Selway permits, but I have never gotten one, never won the lottery. A river runner could spend a lifetime trying and never get a permit. But I like the fact that there is a river as well protected from overuse as the Selway. Maybe it's worth a lifetime of waiting to run a river like that.

A permit to float the Selway River is a most prized possession to a river runner, outranking a Middle Fork or a Grand Canyon permit. Several thousand people a year run the Middle Fork, and you can eventually get on the Grand Canyon.

But the Selway in north-central Idaho is restricted to one launch per day, private or commercial, and trip size is limited to 16 people, including guides. In theory, more than a thousand people a year could run the Selway, but to date no more than 585 have ever done so in a single season due to the vagaries of runoff periods, weather, less-than-maximum party size and happenstance. Two-thirds of the total number go with commercial outfitters, only four of whom have permits to operate on the Selway.

Only a few dozen miles north of the Salmon River, the Selway is more of a Northwest river than the Salmon. Its shoreline is marked by western red cedar and ferns, cascara, buckthorn and red-osier dogwood. One of the original eight wild rivers protected by the National Wild and Scenic Rivers System, the Selway remains the wildest of the wild, both in its wilderness character and in the nature of its rapids. A more technical and demanding river I have not run.

And I have run it legally, even though I haven't had the luck of the draw. Friends of mine have, and I have been fortunate enough to have been invited along on two very different trips: a highwater first-time run and a lowwater run as resident guide—as I was the only one along who had done it before.

The first one grew out of a resolve by a party of Grand Canyon rafters to zero in on a Selway permit. We all applied, and one of us, Taz Talley from North Carolina, was lucky and got his permit the first time he applied. He called, asking if I'd like to join him. You bet I did! We rendezvoused a few months later in Hamilton, Montana, on a rainy day in late June.

I'd just gotten off a week-long Middle Fork trip that involved six days of rain and high water— a survival trip. Was the Selway going to be a repeat? I hoped not, but our drive to the river in the rain was discouraging. We camped in the rain after dark, eating chili for a dismal dinner at Paradise Camp.

By the next morning the rain had stopped, but the river was high. We rigged, loaded and packed while the sun played hide-and-seek through broken cloud cover. By early afternoon the shuttle crew returned and we launched with the river-gauge reading 6 feet, just at the edge of being downright dangerous.

The Selway is an intimate river at the launch site at the mouth of Whitecap Creek. But the first seven miles drop at a rate of 40 feet per mile. It is fast and furious, a busy, rocky route for the first three miles with no rapids as such, then five good rapids in the next three miles: Slalom Slide (Class III), Galloping Gertie (Class II), Washer Woman (Class II), Cougar Bluff (Class II) and Holy Smoke (Class II).

All of them seemed like Class IVs that day, and we took a beating. Especially in Holy Smoke, where we hit huge holes on the left and took on lots of cold water. By the time we reached Running Creek Flat, our intended campsite for the night, we needed a breather and our boats needed bailing. We were ready to rest. At high water, the Selway is a busy river that leaves no time for respite.

Few river campsites are better situated than Running Creek Flat, even though it is immediately across the river from Running Creek Ranch, one of only three obvious intrusions of civilization in the 47-mile roadless Selway corridor. It looks like a small working ranch, but I saw little activity there: a few horses in a corral, deer in the tall grass of the orchard, a small garden, a sprinkler watering a lawn where I saw an albino robin.

The river had dropped ever so slightly by morning, and we felt better about the water level. Launching early, we stopped at the mouth of Running Creek, half a mile downstream on the left, for a hike into the hills that revealed a view downstream as well as a grizzly bear sighting—a young one, perhaps a sign that the great bear is expanding its territory.

Ping Pong Alley (Class II) gave us no trouble. We stopped for lunch at Goat Creek to scout the rapid. The Class III rapid is around an S-bend, a half a mile downstream from Goat Creek. Once it starts, it goes for three-eighths of a mile, a long series of rocky drops and obstacles. When we ran it, the lower end consisted of three plausible slots, but the right-hand run was all but blocked by a jagged tree trunk broken off by some natural force and wedged into the slot.

I have never scouted a rapid more thoroughly. I mapped the series on paper and in my mind, then made a good run, carefully avoiding the right slot at the end. The rapid required plenty of maneuvering to find the best route, considering the necessity of entering the next segment in the right place—technical but not intimidating.

We stopped briefly at Selway Lodge, a second intrusion visible from the river.

None of the rapids below Selway Lodge gave us any trouble as we ran Bear Creek (Class II), Island (Class II) and Rodeo (Class II). We camped that night at Black Sand, but had to find tent sites back in the woods because of the high water. That was the night of the back rubs. Someone complained about sore shoulders and a stiff back. Someone else volunteered to massage her back and shoulders, then someone else started massaging the massager's back and shoulders, and before long there was a complete circle around the campfire—a great night.

We were on the river early the next day. The canyon was still in deep shadow when we ran Pettibone (Class II), which splashed us into alertness. Then we drifted down to Ham Rapid (Class IV), which we tried to scout, but could never find a spot from which we could actually see the rapid. The trail on the right was on so steep a slope we couldn't see the river, and the left bank offered an even less promising observation point. We ran it blind but had no problem.

According to Oz Hawksley, one of the pioneer boaters on the Selway, the rapid got its name when his party had flipped a boat on a high water trip and lost a canned ham. A week later on a repeat trip at lower water, they saw the ham on the bottom of the river, had retrieved it and had it for dinner that night. Thus, Ham Rapid.

We ran all the way down to Moose Creek before we broke out lunch on the rocky point between the Selway and its major tributary. Only then did we realize we'd missed the perfect campsite on the left bank immediately across the river. While we were having lunch, it was occupied by a commercial rafting party that had launched the day after we'd begun our trip.

Going into camp immediately after lunch just downstream on the left, we spent the afternoon scouting the big rapids below the confluence: Double Drop (Class IV), Wa-Poots (Class III), Ladle (Class IV), Little Niagara (Class IV), Puzzle Creek (Class III) and No Slouch (Class III)—all within two and one-half miles. It is as busy a stretch of technical whitewater as I have ever seen. The last five rapids are so close together that it is difficult to enter one if you haven't made a good run in the one above. It is an awesome stretch at any water level, and we were still running at relatively high flow.

It was a long hot afternoon. The trail downstream was on the sunny side of the river, and we stopped a time or two to swim in the clear cool water. Scouting the rapids, we again took careful notes, drew detailed maps and observed critical check-points so we'd remember when to start a move and where to make the hard pull.

Camp was somber that night as we anticipated the next day's challenges. The rattlesnake we'd seen at Ladle Rapid suggested a foreboding symbol. We slept too late to watch the commercials make their run: they were on the river while we were still having our breakfast.

We launched, drifted down to Double Drop and were through it before I realized we were there. I'd missed my check-point, but I made a good run. We all did. Then we ran Wa-Poots, pulling into an eddy above Ladle to reinforce our scout of the previous day. We made more notes, discussed the various possibilities, then Rod led, backing down the tongue to break the eddy wall behind the dome rock at the entrance.

I followed, backing down the chute, breaking across the eddy line to catch the quietwater below the dome rock, then dinking my way down the stair-step series of drops toward the point from which Taz was watching the run. He said later, "Your raft looked like it knew where it was going." I have never made a better run on any rapid, but I had little time to congratulate myself: Little Niagara was immediately downstream waiting to challenge me further.

Ladle was only the first of four rapids within the next mile, all of them tough, but I was in good position to enter the series. It was less an entry than a flush, a steep drop that swept me toward the rock garden I knew I had to avoid to survive. I had to pull hard in the opposite direction, but with two, three deep strokes I was where I wanted to be and hurtling along toward the next rapid, where Rod was already out of sight.

I don't know how many rapids I ran before I spotted Rod in an eddy on the left. I grabbed one on the right, and we waited for Taz, exhilarated by our success. We waited, waited and waited. It must have been 20 minutes before Taz appeared, low in the water but fist in the air, his passengers bailing like mad.

Brimful of water, the raft was all but unmanageable. If anyone but Taz had been at the oars, it would have been a lost cause. An iron-pumper, he is the strongest man I have ever enjoyed a river with, an absolute Atlas, but he was exhausted. We drifted downstream, sharing our runs with each other, each of us having made our own separate peace with the river once we were through Ladle, and flushing down the rest of the course.

Landing on the right bank at what we later learned must have been Cedar Flats, we broke out lunch. Suddenly we were surrounded by butterflies, tiny blues that congregated on the damp beach to suck up moisture. We were all exhausted, drained by the adrenaline surge we had experienced in running the Selway's best rapids.

We ate, skipped rocks, processed our various runs, loafed in the sun—and realized that while we had had no rain on this trip, each day had been cloudy until today. We had been so preoccupied with running the rapids that we'd hardly noticed the weather. It was clear and sunny for the first time since we'd launched. We were thankful for the warmth that dried our dampness left by the cold splashing. It was becoming a great day.

I led after lunch, refusing to be caught in the smoke trailing from Rod's after-lunch cigar, and did a blind run on Osprey, a Class III. Miranda Jane (Class III) was not a problem, nor was Three Links (Class III) a few miles downstream. We drifted with the current, planning to camp at Pinchot. That's where we found the commercial party, which left us no option but to run Wolf Creek (Class IV) late in the day, full of shadow. We scouted it, the trail badly damaged by recent rockfall, from high above as well as at river level.

Rod led, backing down the entry chute to be in a better position to power into the eddy below the guard rock and move across the current. I watched his run from river level, then followed. Taz joined us in the shadows, following his own route.

We camped at Ballinger Creek that last night on the river. Eric and I had to leave early in the morning before the others so we hiked downstream to scout Tee-Kem Falls (Class IV), planned our route and returned to camp in time for dinner. I wrote in my journal: "It's been a clear, sunny day, a real high with all the tough rapids and lovely wilderness—the best river trip ever."

That was before our run out the next morning, which merely confirmed that statement. Up at half past four because both of us had to get back to our jobs, Eric and I witnessed the moon dropping over the ridge to the west as we ate a huge breakfast. Rick and Dean decided to ride down to the head of the rapid with us to watch our run, and Barbara hiked down to photograph.

Just as we launched, the sun burst over the ridge to the east, attacking the mist that rose from the river. Long shadows of ponderosa pine lay across the current and mist, and the world turned to a shadowy green over a mellow river.

We left Rick and Dean on shore in the eddy above the rapid, then ran it with barely a splash in the cool morning. My journal again: "Good run of Tee-Kem, great campsite at Cupboard Creek, good fun rapids, lovely river, an osprey, fish in the deep clear water—a great river."

By 8 o'clock we were off the river, by half past nine we were derigged, packed and loaded for home, already missing the river, suffering cultural shock and dreaming about the next Selway trip.

It came sooner than I'd expected. I gave a slide lecture at the Seattle Aquarium that winter and showed some of my Selway shots.

Afterward a couple came up to talk about the Selway: a friend of theirs had a permit and they wanted to know everything I could tell them about my run. Within a few weeks I'd been invited along as the only person who had actually been on the Selway before.

That second trip began in mid-July. There were 15 of us in seven rafts and a kayak. Water level was low, 1.5 on the gauge at the put-in, barely enough to make the trip. One of the remarkable things about this trip was the wildlife we saw on the drive to the launch site: deer, elk, coyote, marmot, even a mountain lion and three bears, a rubber boa and a crab spider.

The run to Running Creek Flat, where we camped the first night, was more rocky than wet. The Class II rapids were merely Class IIs. We found a cedar waxwing nesting in the camp area and found bear claw marks on an aspen tree in the woods near camp. I remember little of the river until we reached Ham Rapid, which we scouted from the rock at the head of the rapid on the right, then ran. It was a tougher run in low water than in high.

This time we moved into the Tony Point campsite, one of the best on the river and the most frequently used. Again we spent a half a day scouting. The river was very low, especially at Ladle, which is essentially a gigantic rock garden. When we ran it, two boats hung up momentarily; one had to be man-handled through the rocks. We actually ran three different routes through Ladle, the right-hand run, which we'd used in 1986, and two variations of a central route. We camped at Tango Bar and even had a sauna that night.

We reached Wolf Creek late in the day and in deep shadow. This time we had no audience, but the run seemed tougher with so many rocks showing at the entry. Our smallest boat ran a slot on the left to pioneer a different approach. Several of us took a mild beating in a hole or two and were mildly hypothermic when we got into camp at Cupboard Creek, as good a campsite as I'd remembered from my first trip when I'd only observed it from the river.

Generally speaking, the lowwater trip was the easier of the two though we saw more rocks. The flow was more gentle, but some of the rapids were tougher. The fishing was great, and there were more campsites, more sandy beaches. The highwater trip was more challenging, Grand Canyon-big and much more technical.

The Selway is a wilderness river that joins the roadside Lochsa (along U.S. 12 in north-central Idaho) to form the Clearwater, a river that saw the last log run in the West in 1972. The Clearwater is part of the National Wild and Scenic Rivers System along with its Selway source. It was also the river that Lewis and Clark took to the Snake, which ultimately led to the Columbia in 1805 when they finally got out of the mountains after they had been forced by the violent nature of the Salmon River to take an overland route a few dozen miles to the south.

The first river named on the official list of the National Wild and Scenic Rivers System is the Middle Fork of the Clearwater, Its 185 miles include 54 miles of the Selway and 131 of the lower. Selway and the Clearwater. However, the Selway is rarely mentioned: it is simply part of the Clearwater, as far as the official record goes.

But those of us who run rivers know the Selway. We know that it is a wild river, that it is a protected river, that it is a tough river to get a permit to run and a tough river to run once you get on it.

It is also a beautiful river that flows through the living heart of the Selway-Bitterroot Wilderness. The normal run is the 47 miles from just below the mouth of Whitecap Creek, the location of a Forest Service campsite and guard station, to the meadow above the unrunnable Selway Falls. This roadless segment of river is as wild as any I have run, a wilderness renewing itself in the Aldo Leopold sense.

A healthy river flowing through a healthy land, a wild river flowing through a wild land—that's the Selway. It is an inspiring river that challenges not only the skills of the river runner but the policies of a people to keep it wild and to protect it from overuse and from the abuses of civilization.

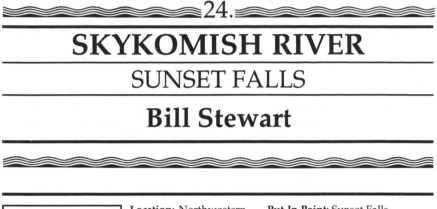

24.

SKYKOMISH RIVER

SUNSET FALLS

Bill Stewart

Location: Northwestern Washington
Whitewater: Class III-IV
River Miles: 4
Gradient: 22 feet per mile
Trip Length: 1 day
Permit Required: No
Contact: Snoqualmie National Forest
Skykomish, WA 98288
(206) 677-2414

Put-In Point: Sunset Falls
Take-Out Point: Railroad Bridge
Access: Skykomish, WA
Land Status: Snoqualmie National Forest

The Sky is running 2,760 cubic feet per second today. The sun is shining, air temperature is 75 degrees and water conditions are favorable for a smooth descent. The lush landscape around me is vibrant and alive. And that's the way I feel today, vibrant and alive. After years of boating the Sky I've discovered that when my mood and the river's mood are in tune, something wonderful can happen. The holes look friendlier, my rolls are sharper, pop-ups more vertical, the landings softer. I have a feeling it's going to be one of those days. As I start the quarter-mile descent to the put-in, a song by the Cars fills my head: "Summer . . . it turns me upside down."

The Skykomish is a day-trip kind of river. Not long enough for overnight camping and broken by a series of falls, it is used primarily by local fishermen and boaters. Commercial rafting companies call it the "premier whitewater run in the state." Though its proximity to

Highway 2 precludes its classification as a wilderness river, it is
nevertheless one of the most beautiful mountain streams in the
country. When the Washington State Scenic Rivers Act was passed
in 1977, the Skykomish was the first and only river included. Ten
years later, legislators are still forming a management plan.

As my kayak and I squeeze through the locked gate blocking
vehicle access to the launch area, the deep monotone of Sunset Falls
becomes audible. I stop at the first viewpoint overlooking the falls.
The river corridor is illuminated in a breathtaking array of blues and
greens. Mount Index and her sister peaks tower more than 5,000 feet
above the river like a scene from a Tolkein novel. The falls roars
below: 104 feet of sheer power pouring over, around and between
huge slabs of granite at a 45-degree pitch. It is difficult to imagine
anyone going through this chaos and emerging in one piece, much
less alive. But amazingly, about half of the unfortunate victims
survive, according to Louie.

Louie is an employee at the truck-and-haul salmon operation at
the base of the falls and knows more than one story of people going
over the falls. Like the guy who slipped at the top while trying to get
a drink of water. Louie happened to watch this one. He saw the
fellow get flung over the gigantic rooster tailwaves in the middle of
the falls and then disappear into the water below. A few seconds
later he was astounded to see the man swimming for shore in the
turbulent water. He threw the man a line and pulled him in.

"Do you want a glass of whiskey?" Louie asked the man.

"No thanks," he replied, "but could I have a drink of water?"

No one since Al Faussett has attempted to navigate the churning
water of the falls on purpose. In 1926, Faussett successfully negotiated the foamy torrent in a 34-foot hand-hewn spruce and canvas
canoe as 3,000 people lined on the banks to watch. Amazingly, he
emerged at the bottom unscathed, his craft still intact, and waved to
the cheering crowd, adding another to his long list of first descents.

Having no inclination toward a second descent, I gladly walk
around the drop today. As I walk past the salmon-holding tank
below the Falls, I see Louie preparing to drop a load of fish into his
specially equipped truck and then haul it four miles upstream to just
above Eagle Falls where a biologist will tag the fish and release them
back into the river. Before the intervention of man, the spawning
used to stop at the falls. The fish could not make the 104-foot jump
to the top. In the 1950s, the Department of Fisheries decided to

influence the run. The agency constructed an expensive and fascinating holding tank complete with a fish elevator. An elaborate log- and debris-filtering system collects the fish below the falls. A biologist then releases them again into the Upper Sky and its tributaries.

Now, 30 years later, thousands of hatchery-raised salmon return here each year, ultimately to find their way to their spawning grounds where they will mate and die. Over the falls, at least, they will get a free ride.

Today the chinook are running, the kings of the salmon clan. As I peer into the 15-foot-deep concrete tank, a 35-pound chinook leaps up the vertical wall and almost makes it over the top. The splash caused by its bellyflop landing douses me. Louie starts the elevator and I watch the magnificent fish rise up to truck level, drop through a tube and disappear into the truck.

The show is over. Louie drives away and I humbly carry my kayak toward the put-in, feeling somewhat disturbed at the blatant and perhaps dubious efforts of man to alter the course of nature.

Like an unpenned salmon I peel out into the Class III waves of Lion's Jaws Rapid. I too have purpose and direction. I am heading for the First Wave at the end of the rapid. But unlike the spawning salmon, the river is taking me downstream. I punch through the wave and coast into the turquoise water of an eddy. It's acrobatics time.

Some days this wave shows up all too quickly. At higher flows it becomes even deeper. On certain days, especially when the air is cold and the sky overcast, the hole can look big, violent and ugly. But today it entices me with its playfulness and I ferry onto it with pleasure. For a few fleeting moments I am frozen, motionless in space and time, while the river and the salmon rush underneath me heading in opposite directions. Suddenly the wave surges. My kayak leaves its horizontal plane and slips into the trough of the wave. The powerful water pushes down the bow and my kayak rises vertically, allowing me to see a clear view of the river before I collapse on my head back into the water.

Several tip-stands later, I pull out and continue downstream, looking forward to a few minutes of peaceful, dry floating. To the unfamiliar, the next rapid can seem intimidating from above. The pour-over at the bottom appears menacing, but experience has taught me that its bark is worse than its bite. I let the river take me at its own pace, occasionally planting a draw or a backstroke to avoid obstacles. For a cheap thrill I drop into the pour-over sideways, bracing onto the following wave and rising over it with ease.

The river slows. I drift lazily along in the current with time to relax and appreciate the view. I'm like a figure in a painting, framed by tree-covered mountains and sandy beaches. Rustic cabins line the river along this section. Though most are vacation properties, a few are inhabited full time by residents of nearby towns like Goldbar or Index.

The picturesque village of Index is nestled three miles away on the North Fork of the Skykomish, which is an action-packed Class IV whitewater run in the spring and late fall. The town was originally homesteaded by Amos Gunn and his family in 1885. Amos Gunn's daughter, Persis, inadvertently named both the town and the mountain when she looked up at the majestic peak and blurted out, "That mountain looks like an index finger!" Gold strikes, and later a railroad, brought people to Silver Creek and Money Creek, and by 1906, Index and the town of Skykomish 18 miles upstream were booming communities. Today, the only thing booming is the river.

I float by the rafting put-in on river left. Around the corner is Garbage Drop, named for its lack of character and its sharp, submerged rocks that can make garbage out of a raft. At this waterlevel most of the rocks are concealed. I drift nonchalantly, and my plastic kayak bounces sharply off a hidden rock. In my Fiberglas boating days I had to be more careful. The transition to plastic has allowed me to become lax about rocks and I remind myself that this is not a healthy attitude. Cable Drop is coming up and I tell myself to pay more attention here.

This rather long Class III–IV rapid is difficult to read from above. The river is obscured by a large boulder in the top center. I glide into the jumbled chute on river left and back-ferry to the center, landing in the breaking wave just below the rock. After a few seconds of hole-riding, I accidently offer the river my upstream edge. The river accepts my offering and swallows the edge, taking me along with it.

I roll up just in time to catch a glassy wave. Surfing back and forth, I lean to avoid getting sucked into the trough and kicked out. I exit the wave and float through the rest of the drop, skirting the series of rather unpleasant holes at the bottom.

As I pass the confluence with the North Fork, the river makes a left-hand turn, the corridor widens and my favorite panorama appears. In front of me is a long, steep Class III boulder garden surrounded by trees. The river seems to disappear into the forest below Mount Index and the mountain stands majestically above like a goddess welcoming me into her domain. Eager to hold this view a little longer, I quickly ferry to a nearby boulder and sweep into the eddy behind. A family of mergansers is already occupying the eddy and they hastily exit the other side as I approach. I watch them scamper gracefully across the Class III ledges, half walking, half swimming, and I find myself wishing I could make the same moves with such a lack of effort.

The pace of the river quickens. After passing Anderson Hole the river drops out of sight, blocked by monstrous boulders that justify a closer look. This is Boulder Drop, respectfully called The Drop by locals. I dutifully eddy out on river right and commence the scouting ritual that great rapids deserve, even though I've run this rapid many times before.

Depending on who is doing the talking, Boulder Drop is either an easy Class V or a Class IV with a little extra punch. It is constantly changing, always difficult and always a league above the rest of the run. I stand on the boulder at the top and gaze at the pickets, a line of boulders in the middle of the rapid. There are two main routes through this chaos: around to the left through the airplane turn or between two of the rocks through a raft-sized slot called the Needle. I decide to run the Needle.

As I prepare to push off I recall a sense of anxiety that used to flow over me at this rapid. In my earlier days that anxiety took the form of mild tremors. Today I am alert and relaxed. The river and I are on the same wavelength.

I drop into the tongue, back-ferry left past the first two holes and eddy out quickly on river right. Phase one complete. Peeling out, I line myself up with the precarious opening. To me, this is the cutting edge of river running. It is too late to ferry across to the relative comfort of the airplane turn run. I am committed to the Needle.

Like a finely honed blade sliding into its sheath, my kayak slips easily over the edge. With my bow pointing at two o'clock, I brace onto the huge but surprisingly soft side-curler at the bottom and the river pushes me left past the dragonback rocks, just where I wanted to be. I continue this course to avoid the recirculating hole in the middle, and my kayak and I bob up and down wildly over the steep roller-coaster waves of the final section.

The bow crosses an eddyline next to the left shore and I let the current whip me around. Slowly moving with the rhythm of the pulsating eddy, I gaze upstream, losing myself in the rapid's power and reflecting on where I've just been and how I got there. On this day a decade ago I was sitting behind a desk in an office without windows, unaware that the Skykomish River existed. Today I am sitting in the front row watching a dazzling natural choreography and feeling good about the route I've chosen.

Possessing renewed energy from a perfect run through Boulder Drop, I break out of the eddy. The ledge is just ahead, a 4-foot drop into a short pool. At higher flows there is a nasty reversal wave formed there. Today, the hydraulic is safe and easy. My boat is lined up with the middle of the chute and I backpaddle to slow myself down. As expected, the downstream jet of water captures my stern and I find myself catching just a glimpse of blue sky overhead before plunging into the azure water of the Sky.

Recovering and moving downstream, I turn around to catch the big, fast waves in Aquagasm. I can feel my downstream progress cease as gravity pushes me down the face of a wave and the ride begins. I quickly get sideways and try to straighten myself out with a rudder stroke, but to no avail. The wave is finished with my antics. It flings me out one end, and I drop behind a boulder in the center of the rapid. Above 3,500 cubic feet per second, this rock creates a dangerous pour-over. Today there is just a semi-calm eddy behind it.

As I relax and regroup, I notice an intriguing wall of water pouring over the left side of the rock. This is worthy of experimentation. I nudge the bow into the wall of water and my kayak is immediately rejected. Like a salmon jumping over the ledge, my kayak leaps from the river. Holding my paddle over my head in a gesture of jubilation, I ride down the river on my bow for what seems an eternity before landing softly upright. With no chance to regain the eddy, I slip downstream, filing the spot away for future reference.

I drift casually through the waves above the railroad bridge take-out, feeling tired yet renewed. It has been a great day on the Sky. I carry my kayak up the hill. As I glance down at the untamed, turquoise water, I notice a salmon jumping in the river below. I feel bonded to the river today, in a special kind of closeness that comes from touching something wild.

25

THE SNAKE RIVER

HELLS CANYON

Verne Huser

Location: Idaho-Oregon Border
Whitewater: Class III-V
River Miles: 79
Gradient: 10 feet per mile
Trip Length: 5 to 7 days
Contact: U.S. Forest Service
Hells Canyon NRA
3620-B Snake River Ave.
Lewiston, ID 83501
(208) 743-2297/743-3648

Permit Required: Yes
Put-In Point: Below Hells
Canyon Dam
Take-Out Point: Hellers Bar
Access: Baker, OR,
Cambridge, ID,
Lewiston, ID, Clarkston, WA
Land Status: Hells Canyon
National Recreation Area

The Snake River of the Northwest, a major tributary of the Columbia, flows more than a thousand miles from its headwaters in northwest Wyoming. Originating in the high country on the boundary of Yellowstone National Park, it snakes through Jackson Hole country past the Teton Range in Grand Teton National Park, then crosses Idaho in a sinuous curve through the great lava flows of ancient times.

The Oregon Trail follows the Snake across southern Idaho, a route thousands took to promised lands during the mid-19th century. Where the Oregon Trail finally leaves the Snake, a place known as Farewell Bend, the river heads north into one of the most rugged landscapes on the continent: Hells Canyon.

Here the Snake forms the boundary between Idaho and Oregon, and farther north, between Idaho and Washington. It also divides two great ranges of mountains, the Seven Devils in Idaho and the Wallowas in Oregon. Hell's Canyon proper lies between the two ranges at a depth half-again as deep as the Grand Canyon, an area that has defied the building of roads. Even today mail is delivered by jetboat along the river.

It is this remoteness that appeals to river runners. It lies in a banana belt where winters are mild and summers are hot enough to scorch bare feet in the hot sand of what beaches are left by the scouring impact of reservoir-release flows that sometimes top 80,000 cubic feet per second for three months to make room in the reservoir for the spring runoff upstream.

There are more that 20 dams on the Snake, three of them in the upper reaches of Hells Canyon itself. But a 79-mile segment from the face of Hells Canyon Dam to the mouth of the Grande Ronde River still runs free. Sixty-seven miles of that segment have been designated as part of the National Wild and Scenic Rivers System; one 31-mile section below the dam has been designated as Wild, and a 36-mile section from Pittsburgh Landing to the forest boundary near the Washington-Oregon state line has been designated as Scenic.

I first discovered Hells Canyon the spring of 1971 on an exploratory trip with Jim Campbell and Hank Miller, two nuclear physicists living in Idaho Falls who were concerned about further threats to dam the Snake again. They established a river-running company, offering raft trips down the Snake through Hells Canyon to let people know what there was to lose to another dam.

We went in mid-April, a perfect time to see Hells Canyon if the weather is fine, which it wasn't. We had rain, but we saw elk and eagles, deer and chukars, and we had some of the finest rapid running that I had known. We were all relatively new to the sport of river running, and at 20,000 cubic feet per second we had our hands full. Jim and Hank had run the river the previous spring and summer; I was the novice, scared out of my wits by the huge boils and eddies, bigger than I'd seen in the Grand Canyon.

We used 27-foot military surplus bridge pontoons with 12- and 13-foot oars, the longer set on the rear mounts, which were slightly wider for better control. On that first run Jim was on the rear oars, I on the front set. While we rigged at the launch site a half-mile below Hells Canyon Dam, the river rushed by with a palpable pulse, swirling and eddying, belching boils and swallowing debris, a powerful river.

When we launched, the pontoon was like a mailbag being caught by a moving train: we pulled into the current, which tried to spit us out, then grabbed us and tried to swallow us. The surge was impressive, even frightening, but then I was relatively a novice; this was my first real whitewater trip at the oars.

At Wild Sheep Rapid some five miles downstream we stopped to scout. By then I'd had a chance to learn a little about the power of the river and I was still slightly terrified. I was used to the placid Snake in Jackson Hole, where I'd been guiding for a decade. This was new to me.

Wild Sheep is an impressive rapid at 20,000 cubic feet per second. We studied it for half an hour, then Jim pulled me aside to explain our route through the maelstrom: "I want to be two oar-lengths from that rock wall," he said, a point he repeated three or four times as we made our way back to the boat. We tied everything in, adjusted our life jackets and rowed into the eddy above the drop. The eddy carried us upstream a hundred yards, giving us ample time to row out into the river and cross the current to the opposite side. We had scouted on the left, and were running it on the right—two oar-lengths from the right-hand shore.

What a flush! We were through in less time than it takes to tell it, riding the tailwaves to glory, pulling into the eddy below and signaling our success. Hank and Sharon, the first woman licensed to guide river trips in Idaho, followed. They'd just been married; this was something of a honeymoon trip for them.

No one pays much attention to the rapids above Wild Sheep, even though they are rated as Class III—Cliff Mountain, Brush Creek, Rocky Point. Wild Sheep and Granite Falls are the biggies, and all respect seems to be reserved for them, though the little ones sometimes sneak up on you. Haystacks, another Class III halfway between Wild Sheep and Granite, gave us a wetting that day but nothing worse. We camped at Granite Creek, which became our standard campsite for years, until a bear problem developed. A camper was attacked and the bear was destroyed.

I have never liked calling the next rapid Granite because Granite Creek has nothing to do with it. There is a little rapid at Granite Creek, but the creek has no appreciable impact on the river at the major rapid a quarter-mile below, the one listed as Granite Falls. Its location at the mouth of Cache Creek suggests an alternate name, and many early river runners referred to it as Cache Creek Rapid, but usage generally wins out over logic, so it is known as Granite today.

It is an impressive rapid. Les Jones, the early river-running map maker, rates Granite right up there with Lava Falls and Hance in the Grand Canyon. Rod Nash and Bob Collins included Granite in *The Big Drops.* It was big enough for me, especially on that first trip.

We ran it on the right, hitting the diagonal wave from the right as straight on as we could. That is, we tried to anticipate the impact of the wave on the bow and calculate the angle of the pontoon to the current against that impact. We made a good run that day—after scouting it three times during our overnight at Granite Creek: we'd hike down, study the rapid, examine the old pictographs on the rock wall just above the rapid, go back to camp and return to study the rapid again.

I once broke an oar in Granite, and I still believe the end of the oar hit the bottom of the river. There were two groups on the river at the same time. The one just ahead of us flipped a pontoon. A runner was sent back upstream to warn us away from running the right-hand slot that had flipped them, but the message missed its point: all the messenger delivered were the facts of the flip without a warning.

When we ran it, I was on the rear set of oars, my wife on the front ones. As we approached the drop—the river was running at 14,000 cubic feet per second—I misjudged the lateral currents. Instead of hitting the lateral wave head-on, we hit it largely broadside. It stopped us cold, tilted us at a sharp angle and threw us into the trough formed by the wave. It was then that my left oar snappe;, I'm certain it hit a rock on the bottom of the river—or the riverbed itself. The impact seemed to spring us back out of the hole, and my wife, still pushing two good oars, kept us on course as we wallowed through, riding the tailwaves into the eddy, happy to be upright.

Below Granite there is a series of 10 rapids of Class III or Class IV in the next dozen miles; below that, hardly anything for more than 20 miles. The action is all in the first 18 miles. Below Johnsons Bar, the upriver limit of most jetboats, there are plenty of eddies and boils, frightening at times but manageable. There used to be wonderful sandy beaches below Granite—I remember them myself—but now they have all been washed away by the high flows controlled by the dam-operators as they spill water to make room in the reservoir for the spring runoff.

Only at Salt Creek is there a reasonable beach. Below Granite the river flows through its deepest canyon, but at Johnsons Bar it opens up a bit: you can see Hat Point on the Oregon side and even the top of the Seven Devils on the Idaho side. Below Johnsons Bar lies another short canyon. Then the river runs into Suicide Point, eddies left and into a big bend as Salt Creek comes in from the left, just below Temperance Creek Ranch, a working sheep operation the last time I ran Hells Canyon.

The beach at Salt Creek has been formed by a huge eddy. For almost a mile on the left bank there is a massive layer of sand, full of rattlesnakes and cactus. Three crescent beaches have been carved by the river out of the massive sand deposit, itself left by an earlier and bigger river. They're a great place to camp, and to swim and are the only sandy beaches until you reach the mouth of the undammed Salmon.

On later trips down the Snake, I began to notice other aspects of the canyon: the wildflowers and the birds, the vegetation in general and the fauna. Ernest Hemingway's son Jack convinced me that there were fish in the river. It had been too muddy all spring to even consider fishing, but Hemingway, using black-haired wet flies, was catching bass at the mouths of tributary creeks.

When I began guiding regularly in the spring and summer of 1972, I got to know the river in many different moods. In 1971 I'd seen it between 17,000 and 80,000 cubic feet per second, a high runoff year. On one trip the river rose from 20,000 cubic feet per second at launch to 80,000 by the time we were camped at Johnsons Bar, where we had to get up at least twice during the night to re-tie the boats. Had we left them tied to their initial mooring, we'd have had to dive into 6 feet of water in the morning to untie them.

The winter of 1971 to 1972, I spent a lot of time in Hells Canyon, and saw 82,000 cubic feet per second spilled for three months to make room in the reservoirs for the snowpack at runoff time. But when summer arrived, we were running on between 5,000 and 17,000 cubic feet per second. The lowest water I'd seen in 1971 was the highest water I saw in 1972. The river changes tremendously at different waterlevels.

I remember running a trip when we'd been experiencing 20,000 cubic feet per second for several days and the river had a "bathtub ring" of several vertical feet between the high-water scouring mark and river level. As we approached the mouth of the Salmon River, the bathtub ring suddenly disappeared. Something was blocking the Snake, damming it and raising its level. When we reached the confluence with the Salmon, we found it running wild, a flow of 98,000 cubic feet per second, we later learned. The flow of the undammed Salmon was actually backing water up the Snake.

Below the Salmon the flow was in the neighborhood of 120,000 cubic feet per second with a force that carried us at a rate of eight miles an hour, as fast as I have ever moved on a river by muscle and river power.

We used to pan for gold in Hells Canyon, digging into the sand at known sites and washing the show of color from the debris. We'd stop and explore the old mine at the confluence with the Imnaha, visit the hydraulic mining site where an ancient pump had pulled water from the Snake to wash gold from the bank, and visit Eureka Bar where the foundation of the old mill still remains high above the river. We found eye-bolts, huge ones, used by the steamboats for winching up the rapids, and we saw inscriptions left by prehistoric Indians, Chinese miners, and early inhabitants of Hells Canyon.

Numerous old homesteads remained in Hells Canyon in those days. Some are gone now, a few of them burned, while others have been vandalized. The number of jetboaters has increased geometrically in the canyon and river runners have increased too. The lower end of Hells Canyon is an absolute zoo on weekends.

My last trip through Hells Canyon was an early October run that saw us launching early Monday morning and pulling off the river Saturday at noon. We saw virtually no one else on the river all week until Friday afternoon when the jetboats started running upstream from the Lewiston-Clarkston area.

I've been on the Snake in Hells Canyon in almost each of the months, boating or hiking or camping. The winter of 1971 to 1972 I visited the river above Wild Sheep with Jim Zanelli, who ran jetboat trips on that stretch below Hells Canyon Dam. There was a moose in the canyon that winter, a young bull that had wandered in from somewhere, and we went in to have a look at him. He was gone by spring when we started running river trips.

Zanelli and I became friends that winter even though we were, in a sense, rivals on the river. His wife, Doris, did the shuttle for me on several river trips that I ran. They were killed flying back from a river trip in their small plane, crashing within view of their home near Oxbow in Hells Canyon.

My wife and I were married in Hells Canyon the spring of 1972 on the Oxbow Promontory overlooking the Snake River in Hells

Canyon only a mile or two from Zanelli's home. Ah, the memories that flood back: backpacking down the west side of Hells Canyon Reservoir, bird watching that spring along the river where lazuli buntings and Lewis woodpeckers were so abundant, feeding hay to the wintering mule deer that had lost their winter range to the reservoirs, seeing a cougar cross the road ahead of my car at Pine Creek.

Hells Canyon has been with me for 16 1/2 years as of this writing. It has changed much in those years, but the river is still there, alive and well—as alive and well as a river can be that has been harnessed as frequently as has the Snake. Along with the 20 dams above, there are eight dams downstream from Hells Canyon—four on the lower Snake and four on the Columbia. It is a hard-working river.

But there are still salmon and steelhead and sturgeon in the Snake; deer, elk, bear and chukars abound in the surrounding forests and active sheep and cattle industries still thrive in the canyon. There is less logging now, perhaps because of the wilderness designations, but Hells Canyon is too steep, too remote for a healthy timber industry.

The Snake itself still flows, when reservoir releases let it, through the mighty canyon that it carved over the centuries. There will be no more dams if Wild and Scenic river designation means anything, and if there is ever any real control over the jetboaters as there is over the downriver recreational users, the Snake will still be a place to find solitude, to discover the peace and quiet of the natural world.

Hells Canyon of the Snake still thrills me, and I want to go back and run it again, in the spring when green velvet time comes again and the wildflowers riot on the sunny slopes above the rapids. I want to scout Wild Sheep and Granite, run Waterspout on the left and cheat the eddies off Suicide Point, fish for steelhead at the mouth of the Imnaha, camp on the sandy beaches below the mouth of the Salmon, drink water from the falls at Cherry Creek. Is it still safe?

26.

THE TUOLUMNE RIVER

MERAL'S POOL TO WARD'S FERRY

Paul Hoobyar

Location: Central California
Whitewater: Class III–V
River Miles: 18
Gradient: 40 feet per mile
Trip Length: 1 to 3 days
Permit Required: Yes
Contact: Stanislaus National Forest
Groveland Ranger District
P.O. Box 709, Groveland, CA 95321
(209) 962-7825

Put-In Point: Meral's Pool
Take-Out Point: New Don Pedro
Reservoir and Ward's Ferry Rd.
Access: Groveland, CA
Land Status: National Wild and
Scenic Rivers System

Sitting like a serrated ridgebone along California's eastern flank, the Sierra Nevada Mountains create a huge, natural reservoir. Virtually an impenetrable wall for the storms moving in off the Pacific Ocean, this spine of mountains is volcanic in origin, formed along a fault zone. The latest thinking purports that the Sierras were born of pressures created from the plates of the earth's ocean-basin crust sliding under the edge of the North American continent. The rivers carving and sculpting these mountains are products of this pregnant watershed, creating precipitous canyons and steep drainages.

As western civilization has populated the area, this natural reservoir has been developed to the extent that today no river basins remain in the Sierra Nevada's void of hydrologic development. "Rivers" in the Sierras today are only remnants of their original identities that flow between flumes and reservoirs.

160

One such section in the central Sierras is on the Tuolumne River. This 18-mile long stretch above the New Don Pedro Reservoir still displays its original rollicking habits along a streambed that averages a 40-foot-per-mile elevation drop. Sitting only 150 miles east of the San Francisco Bay Area, this river is one of the most popular in California and the West Coast because of its whitewater, its scenery, its native trout fishery and its undeveloped canyon. In fact, the river is so popular and respected that it became part of the National Wild and Scenic Rivers Act in 1984 after a 10-year battle to save it from further hydro-development.

A group of us decided to meet on the Tuolumne for a spring run in April. The *really* big runoffs hadn't occurred yet, and with that great combination of warm weather and ample water so typical to the central Sierra foothills in spring, we met at Lumnsden Campground for a two-day sport down the T.

Driving down the bumpy, dirt surface of Lumsden Road, I thought about the cattle drives in and out of the canyon along this same road every spring and fall—a tradition dating back to the turn of the century. The car creaked and groaned into the canyon and the road enforced a speed approximating those cattle herds. After the three-hour highway blitz up from the Bay Area, I appreciated leaving behind the manic pace of the 20th century as we dropped farther down into the canyon.

The road twisted, bumped and slid downhill. As it made a final swoop near the river, we saw the first rapid through the windshield. Watching 4,500 cubic feet per second slamming their way around and over Rock Garden Rapids, the juice started coursing through my veins.

While the shuttle was being run, a couple of boaters hiked up the road to run the rapids below Lumnsden Falls. A mile and a half lies between the put-in and the falls, and they planned to hike as far as their bare feet would allow before hopping into their boats. Since it was my first run of the season, I opted to put in at Meral's Pool and run the traditional stretch.

After the ritual warm-up of rolls and braces, we pushed off for the negative ions below. The first two miles of the T packed a wallop of whitewater in five major drops. I casually dropped into a "small" hole in Nemesis, the second rapid on the run, and after "window-shading" three times in the keeper, I stabilized on the brace and backed out through a side exit. Whew! As I slid into an eddy to drain the backs of my eyeballs, Pat, sitting innocently watching, asked, "Do you always test holes that way, Paul?"

Despite the canyon's beauty, the river's whitewater display stole center stage. My attention was riveted to the water as we paddled. Pour-overs, holes and haystacks glistened, pulsating in the sun. The river kept us dancing and playing while we moved downstream. As I sponged out my boat in an eddy, my eyes followed the contours of the canyon walls opposite me. The familiar yellow pine populated the rocky slopes, but I was more intrigued with the ancient digger pines jutting out of the hillside at different angles. These trees, with their arthritic trunks and airhead crowns, are characteristic of the Central Sierras.

The conifer's name was bequeathed by the early white settlers as a reference to the hills, original inhabitants. Diggers, or Miwok Indians, inhabited this area for nearly 2,000 years before the white man came, taking part of their sustenance from roots and bulbs. In the mid-1800s, the 49er gold rush attracted whites into the area, and the Miwoks were inhospitably turned out of the canyon. Remains of gold mines still dot the canyon walls.

My eyes continued up to the ridge tops. The slice of blue sky overhead was punctuated by tufts of cumulus clouds skating above the canyon rims. The sun blazed golden-warm in contrast to the cold, clear water of the Tuolumne.

We leapfrogged our way down to Clavey Falls, the bull-buck chunk of whitewater on this run. The Clavey River joins the Tuolumne right above the falls, and the confluence is a popular lunch and camp site. The falls is a main attraction, but the Clavey River is an attraction in its own right. Fossilized horn coral was discovered near the confluence of the two rivers in 1974. Considered a rare geological find, this is one of only two documentable fossil sites known in the entire Calaveras Formation, which underlies much of the western Sierra foothills. At lower water flows, people hike up the Clavey for long sits in the jacuzzi-like pools or frolic in the water slides carved out of the bedrock. In mid-April, however, the boisterous Clavey River doesn't invite such intimate excursions, and I never could make lunch a very attractive thought at the top of a major drop.

Clavey Falls is formed by a weir of chert (a form of quartz) extending across the entire streambed, with rocks, boulders and holes dotted below the first pour-over. A standard run is to start left over the initial ledge and veer right, missing the big hole against the far left wall at the bottom of the rapid. Like any popular major rapid, though, Clavey Falls has been run innumerable ways. I threaded a needle between two boulders at the bottom of a sharp pour-off on the center right, then eddied out to see where the rest of the group ran.

Below Clavey Falls the river calmed down, and, as the adrenaline left my veins, the fatigue of the last six miles of hectic paddling and playing weighed like lead in my arms. Powerhouse campsite, the night's lodging, was only two miles away, and we floated quietly down to camp. After tents were set up and the evening meal was started, we poked around in the old building's foundations, looking at the fittings and pipes, imagining what the structure must have looked like.

The powerhouse that sat on the old foundation was reportedly built in 1905 to 1906 by a couple of ambitious, marginally successful entrepreneurs who hoped to sell electricity to the mining operations working along the T. The Tuolumne Electric and Transmissions Company operated the powerhouse until it was sold, sometime after 1910. Unused after 1914 due to the decline of gold mining and the powerhouse's outdated systems, a major fire in 1928 destroyed most of the building. A flood finished the job in 1937.

Thanks to the Tuolumne's inclusion in the Wild and Scenic Rivers Act, no further hydroelectric structures will be built within the river canyon, making the remains of the "aught-five" powerhouse quaint and entertaining to peruse. In California, the consensus among lovers of wild rivers is that the loss of the nearby Stanislaus River, due to filling of the reservoir behind the New Melones Dam in 1981, set the stage for saving the Tuolumne. Once the City and County of San Francisco and two local Central Valley irrigation districts made serious bids to impound the rest of the Tuolumne River, the freedom fighters for the Tuolumne went to work and created a broad-based, grass-roots coalition of fishing anglers, boaters, nature and wildlife lovers and local politicians to oppose further development of the T's hydropower potential. This piece of water is here for our children and grandchildren to enjoy. That thought gave me warmth as the chill night air descended into the canyon and darkness enveloped the surrounding hills.

The next morning we broke camp early and pressed down to Gray's Grindstone, a three-quarter-mile-long rapid with a big elevation drop and lots of hydraulics to dodge or dive into at bigger water flows, depending on your a boater's inclination. About two-thirds of the way down the rapid, a big hole stretched off the right bank and sits gnashing and beckoning—a fun sight in the middle of any long rapid. Some of the paddlers in our group dropped into the hole to get a taste of the Grind before heading off downstream.

Toward the bottom end of the run, Steamboat Rapid delays many paddlers from making an early take-out. At certain waterlevels, the hole in Steamboat can be perfect for playing and practice, due to its large size and open ends. At lower flows, the hole is very pronounced, and many a California kayaking hotdogger has been known to polish his "big-hole riding" skills here. A large rock outcropping extends off the river's right bank, and we took turns jumping into the hole and then stretching out on the bedrock overlooking it for the revitalizing warmth of sun and earth. Nose stands, tail stands, cartwheels, pirouettes and endos flashed out of Steamboat Rapid in the morning sunlight. A few swims toward the end of our play belied the fatigue we all felt as we finally headed downstream.

Below Steamboat, Cabin and Hell's Kitchen rapids held little interest for our tail-dragging group. We slid under the remains of an old suspension bridge marking the location of some extensive goldmining operations in this part of the canyon. The Mohican and Mary Ellen miners searched for the "Mother Lode" during the same goldcrazed period as the rest of the canyon (1850 to 1900), and ruins can still be seen on both sides of the river.

The North Fork of the Tuolumne joins the main flow of the T below the old suspension bridge, and shortly downstream of that we encountered the flotsam that collects at the top of New Don Pedro Reservoir. Driftwood, styrofoam and other things not so easily recognized (nor desired for recognition) choke the waters here.

Somewhere underneath all that flotsam and water, I knew a rock pile exists named Pinball Rapids that periodically sees the light of day in late summer and fall when the reservoir is down. As we hiked our kayaks to the cars, I pictured the rapid like a hibernating Sasquatch, biding its time until its next call to action. When Pinball's at large, the river-wide ledge and boulder field send all boaters into the placid reservoir beyond with 220 volts of adrenaline zapping through their limbs: the Tuolumne's ultimate closing act.

27.

THE YAMPA RIVER

YAMPA CANYON

Jeff Rennicke

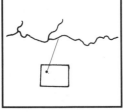

Location: Northwestern Colorado

Whitewater: Class II-III

River Miles: 46

Gradient: 11 feet per mile

Trip Length: 2 to 3 days

Permit Required: Yes

Put-In Point: Deerlodge Park

Take-Out Point: Echo Park

Access: Steamboat Springs, CO
Jensen, UT, Vernal, UT

Land Status: Dinosaur National Monument

Contact: National Park Service, Dinosaur National Monument
P.O. Box 210, Dinosaur, CO 81610
(303) 374-2216

It can be one of the most graceful combinations in all of nature—and one of the most powerful. Water and rock. Deep in the slickrock country of northwestern Colorado there is a canyon where both the beauty and the brute force of that combination are laid bare.

It is a complex, contradictory landscape. The maps wear names like Happy Canyon and Disappointment Draw, Starvation Valley and Thanksgiving Gorge, Dry Woman Canyon and Five Springs Draw. Summers are hot with a sun that can melt your belt buckle and with sky the color of blue flame. Winters are dry and windy enough to rid a man of his whiskers. It is a big country where a person can lose his or her shadow, and echoes ring off the slickrock until you grow tired of listening. And, through its heart flows a river.

The river is as wild and unruly as the land it flows over. The spring floods that this river has carried on its back have carved a canyon 2,500-feet deep that winds as twisted and tangled as a dropped lariat. With sidecanyons polished slick as marble, driftlogs like old bones lodged high on ledges, groves of cottonwood far from the river and scoured the color of old barn wood by the highwater mark, it is a river that carries its threat of flash flood like a loaded six-gun. When it cut this canyon it carried no name. Early maps called it The Bear and today that name still lingers on the tongues of some of the old-timers. But to most, it is known as a Ute Indian word for a plant that was used as food and was also said to have certain other powers. Loosely translated, the word means "big medicine." The river is called the Yampa.

Our five rafts drift away from Deerlodge Park, the launch area for a Yampa River trip, and the ghostly cottonwood grove toward Yampa Canyon where the "big medicine" of the river begins.

Today the Yampa River is wild, raging at nearly 14,000 cubic feet of water per second, the largest free-flowing tributary in the Colorado River Basin. It is the last of a breed. In the 1950s it became the focal point of the national conservation movement when the proposed Echo Park Dam at the river's mouth was defeated loudly. But the attention has faded and although the Yampa has been recommended for inclusion in the Wild and Scenic Rivers System, it remains unprotected and vulnerable.

Flowing as it does near one of the West's largest deposits of oil shale, the dam proposals did not stop with the defeat at Echo Park. Two new dams, this time upstream in the narrow gorges of Juniper and Cross Mountain canyons, are being considered to create a reservoir 90 miles long that would still the pulse of the last wild river in the basin.

But on this early morning in early June with the mist still hanging over the water and the river flowing with another of its springtime floods, the canyon looks much the same as it must have looked to early explorers. Although Nathaniel Galloway and his son Parley are most often cited with the maiden voyage on the river in 1909, there is some evidence that a man once described as "gentle as a child when used rightly, a wounded grizzly when provoked" may have beaten them to it. James Baker was not a man to keep much in the way of records beyond a few notches in his gunbelt, but in a report given to river historian Robert Brewster Stanton in 1907 by Jack Sumner, the head boatman for the first Powell Expedition, it is said that Baker and a companion "went in bull-boats down the Bear River

Canyon to the Green and down the Green to Kelly's Hole" (today called Island Park). No date is given, but since Baker died in 1898, his exploration must have predated Galloway's by at least a dozen years.

A first descent wouldn't amount to much to a man like Nathaniel Galloway, a quiet mountain man who wilderness historian Otis Marston has called "one of the greatest outdoorsmen and boatmen of them all." He is a man remembered more for *how* he ran the rivers than for when. I think of Galloway as I spin the boat downstream, letting it drift the first few quiet miles of the river.

In Galloway's day it was the practice of boatmen to row through rapids with their backs to the danger, giving them leverage but poor visibility. It was a technique that resulted in many campfire stories and splintered boats. Galloway decided that the loss of power by facing forward into a rapid was more than compensated for by the ability to see. So he turned around. It was a simple and yet radical move that took river running out of the Stone Age and brought it into the modern age. Boating became less of a battle with the river and more of a ballet. Even today a boatmen rowing bow first into a rapids is said to be using "the Galloway position."

The first miles of the Yampa below Deerlodge Park require only enough boating skill to spin the boat toward one view or another of the canyon walls. For 10 miles we drift, watching the patterns of stripes called "desert varnish" where minerals that have washed over the cliff faces have stained the light sandstone with intricate webbings like the lines of a charcoal sketch: nature working with a small brush.

Then there is a faint roar, like wind through the piñons. It grows louder. At Teepee Rapid, the artistry turns to power. Here, the river speeds up and begins a drop of 70 feet over the next two and a half miles. It is classic desert canyon whitewater formed by rocks tumbled into the river by sidecanyon floods, rolling and spirited. It is what Earl Perry, the lead boatman on this trip and river ranger for the Yampa, calls "exhilarating but forgiving."

Not far below Teepee Rapid, water and rock have come together to form a very different kind of artistry. High on the cliff walls there are strange pinnacles like the pillars of some long-vanished castle. They are called hoodoos and there are hundreds of them throughout slickrock country, standing like sentinels guarding the canyons and their secrets of time. In the slanted light of late afternoon, the shadow of a hoodoo points downstream to our camp.

The campsites on the Yampa River have been a source for many heated campfire discussions. Not because of the fact that they are assigned by a ranger before the trip, but for their role in the wilderness of the river. Each major site has a steel fire grate, a picnic table, and developed outhouse—creature comforts in a land of few creatures. Most river runners feel that the "improvements" give the riverbank the feel of a roadside campground. River managers feel the facilities lessen the impact of high use and so improve the wilderness feeling. The debate will likely require many more campfires to resolve.

Around our campfire just upstream from Big Joe Rapid, we talk of hoodoos and rapids and wild rivers. A free-flowing river like the Yampa is a maverick in a world of dams and diversions. Its headwaters and source are clouds, rain and snow, not some dial-controlled turbine in a dam. The bends and curves of a wild river like the Yampa orchestrate life in the canyon like the rise and fall of a conductor's baton. When all the rivers are dammed, the music will stop.

The music of Big Joe Rapid sings all night through our dreams. At daybreak, it is an enjoyable ride with the river running high, just the swells of the water flexing its muscles. At Big Joe the rock seems to lighten and the canyon becomes more airy as the Weber sandstone begins to dominate. It is through this rock formation that the river once again becomes an artist.

It begins a mile or so below Harding Hole and winds like a rattlesnake. At Serpentine Bends the Yampa becomes a river with time on its hands, winding back and forth for seven river miles, covering less than two miles as the raven flies.

The canyon seems still and silent as we wind around the bends, hearing only the call of a raven, a sound like cracking rock. There is an abundance of wildlife living along the river—deer, mountain lion, coyote—and the high ledges of the cliffs might show the nests of the endangered peregrine falcon. It is one of the fastest birds on wing, reaching over 100 miles an hour when diving on its prey. But the heat of the day makes the canyon quiet and still. Few things except humans, move in the canyons during the hot sun.

Humans have been moving in the canyon for a long time. Most rugged canyons have their own cast of desperados, hermits and rough company, and the Yampa is no exception. In the late 1870s, when a down-and-out Civil War veteran by the name of Pat Lynch found himself in sudden need of solitude, he lit out for the Yampa.

In several locations in the canyon Lynch lived a solitary life until 1917, a free man along a free river. In a cave filled with Indian artifacts along the river, Lynch left a written note asking others, in less than perfect grammar:

> If in these caverns you shelter take
> Please do them no harm
> Lave everything you find around
> Hanging up or on the ground.

The warning must have worked, for several important archaeological finds have been made along the river, including a leather pouch containing 350 flicker feathers and a headdress made of mule deer hide with the ears of the animal still attached. Lynch himself was buried along the river and his grave was only recently discovered.

The change is sudden. It is difficult to say exactly where it happens, but it is somewhere near Tiger Wall, a huge overhanging wall striped with desert varnish. It begins with an old tradition that calls for one of the women on the trip to kiss Tiger Wall three times as her boat floats by to insure good fortune in what lies below: Warm Springs Rapid.

It is the knowledge of Warm Springs that causes the change, the sudden silence among the boatmen. For more than 40 miles the Yampa has shown the artistry of rock and water. We are about to come face-to-face with the power.

Like several major western rapids, Warm Springs is the product of violence, an immense flash flood that ripped the throat out of a sidecanyon on June 10, 1965, slamming rocks so violently against the canyon walls that huge slabs were knocked off and into the river. For a time, the debris formed a natural dam, stopping the river in its tracks until the water built up enough to push on. Warm Springs was born.

To get a look at the rapid, you hop like an insect among the huge boulders rolled down the sidecanyon like buckshot by the flood. To walk among the house-sized boulders, which still show the raw, white scars where they were cracked by the force, is a lesson in the power of water. And then there is the rapid.

There is little to discuss, really. There is only one sound run at this waterlevel, but scouting is a kind of homage to the river. The run is to the right, pulling away from the ragged heart of the waves. All five of our boats come through cleanly.

Since Warm Springs is such a young rapid, it is still settling, and highwater years have changed it dramatically, making the passage a bit more safe. Still, it is the most awesome rapid in Dinosaur National Monument, and the sight of it and those boulders lining the shore where the flood dropped them that night in 1965, is evidence of the power of water.

Warm Springs is just four miles from the Yampa's confluence with the Green River, the end of the line, at Echo Park. Deep beneath the cliffs of Echo Park there is a gravel bar of willows and river-polished rock, the hieroglyphics of heron tracks in the mud. Sitting at the edge of that gravel bar it is possible, within the reach of your arms, to trail your hands in two great rivers at once—the Yampa from the east and the Green from the north. Both rivers have come a long way to this point from their headwaters in distant mountains. The waters of both rivers carry the colors of their canyon walls. At certain times of the year both rivers flow with the same force and strength. But there is a difference, and with your hands in the two rivers at once you can feel it like a pulse: the Yampa is wild.

DOWNSTREAM
Jeff Rennicke

The moment shatters like glass. From around the corner, out of a cleft in the cliffs, the take-out suddenly swings into view. The trip is nearly over. No one is talking. No one is paddling. The oars rest heavily against my hands as we drift slowly toward the end of another trip.

There is a sadness inherent in the ending of a river trip. Untying the knots and pulling the gear off a raft is like taking down the Christmas tree. Something good is coming to an end. Even if it has done nothing but rain for a solid week, even if the spaghetti dinner got sand in it when the wind came up, even if the cooler is down to nothing but *lite* beer, there is a feeling of panic in the pit of your stomach when the take-out nears.

For a day or a week or a month you have slipped into another dimension, river time: a slower and more sane pace where there are only three times of day—sunrise, lunch and the campfire. For a moment you are not quite sure what day it is and that white stripe on your wrist where the watch used to be is now tanned and brown. Your car keys have slipped to the bottom of the riverbag and all the money in your wallet is damp and seems foreign and silly. For the first time you notice the sand in your shoes and it doesn't seem to matter.

Wild rivers are more than just pathways of water from here to there. They are as much pathways into ourselves. There is no rushing a river. When you go there, you go at the pace of the water and that pace ties you into a flow that is older than life on this planet. To drift on a river is to see time pass in a cadence that is ancient and understandable. Acceptance of that pace, even for a day, changes us and reminds us of other rhythms beyond the sound of our own heartbeats. Stepping off the boat at the take-out starts the clocks to ticking again. So we drift, stretching each moment until it seems it would snap.

Every year in the West more than a million people come to the water's edge to run rivers, ride rapids, float quietwaters, sit around campfires and, finally, drift slowly toward the take-out. There is always the feeling that perhaps we should just keep going, drift right on by the take-out and follow the river around the next bend and the next until it doesn't go any more, until the water tastes like salt and the current blows itself out like a spent wind. Who can say if there will ever be the chance again? There are appointments to keep, bills to pay. And who can say if the river will even be there next time? Even with the National Wild and Scenic Rivers System, our rivers are being dammed and diverted at a faster pace than they are being preserved. *Lite* beer or not, we should just keep going. But we don't.

At the take-out, it looks like a bomb has exploded as gear is strewn across the rocks to dry and be sorted. Addresses are exchanged, one last story told. And then they are gone. I am always the last to leave. With the rafts rolled and the kayaks secured on top of the truck, I walk back to the river once more and toss a branch far out into the current. For a long time I stand there watching, seeing it dancing among the waves until it floats off and disappears around the bend, downstream.

ABOUT THE AUTHORS

Jeff Rennicke is the author of several books, including the *Bears of Alaska* and *The Rivers of Colorado*. He is a contributing editor to *Canoe* magazine and a contributing writer to *River Runner*. He also writes for *Backpacker*, *Outdoor America* and *Explore*. He is an outdoorsman, professional boatman and a guide on the rivers of the American West and Alaska. Between river trips and writing assignments, he lives in Boulder, Colorado.

David Bolling has been rafting and kayaking the rivers of the West since 1974. The addiction developed during the decade-long battle to save the Stanislaus River and has carried him down a lot of rivers and through many river preservation battles. He is a frequent contributor to *River Runner* and is currently at work on a novel about the ill-fated Stanislaus battle. He is the executive director of Friends of the River, a river conservation organization.

Brian Clark is a writer and photographer who lives on a farm in Northern California. For a decade he has paddled, taught kayaking and captured the beauty and thrills of rivers in words and pictures. The search for whitewater has taken him to rivers such as the Bio Bio, the Apurimac, the Urubamba and the Jatate in Latin America, down the Zambezi in Africa and down many of the rivers in the American West. His writing and photography appear in such publications as *Outside, River Runner, Canoe* and many newspapers across the country.

Robert C. "Bert" Gildart is a full-time freelance writer and photographer who lives in Kalispell, Montana. His work has appeared in many national and international publications including *Smithsonian, Travel & Leisure* and *Field & Stream*. Assignments have taken him throughout much of North America and Europe. He is a veteran rafter who has floated many rivers throughout the Northwest.

Paul Hoobyar has run rivers in Canada, Mexico, Central America and Europe, as well as the United States. He has made first descents of rivers in North and Central America by kayak. As a river guide, Hoobyar has worked on many rivers of the West. As an author he published his first works in 1982 and has since become a contributing editor for *Canoe*.

Verne Huser is one of the most prolific natural history writers in America. For more than 30 years he has been a defender of our wilderness areas and wild rivers. With five books, including his most recent work, *River Reflections*, and hundreds of magazine articles, Huser has opened the world of rivers to an entire generation of paddlers. He is the senior contributing editor and book editor of *River Runner* magazine and is currently working on a book entitled *Canoe Routes: Western Washington*.

Larry Rice works for the Marshall State Fish and Wildlife Area in Lacon, Illinois. He is a contributing editor for *Canoe*. His paddling has brought him to such places as Patagonia, Alaska, Canada and to many campsites along rivers and lakes in the West and the North. His writing and photography appear frequently in such publications as *Sierra, Alaska, Backpacker* and *River Runner*.

Bill Stewart is a founder of the Northwest Outdoor Center based in Seattle, Washington, and is an avid whitewater and ocean kayaker. In his younger days he had to drive 10 hours from his Indiana home to seek out prime whitewater. The search brought him to many rivers across North America including the Nantahalla, the Ocoee and the Colorado through the Grand Canyon. Most recently he traveled to Costa Rica to extend his search. Having acquired the wisdom that comes with age and countless miles spent doing shuttles, Stewart now lives within a hour's drive of some of the best paddling the Northwest has to offer.